THEN COME BACK

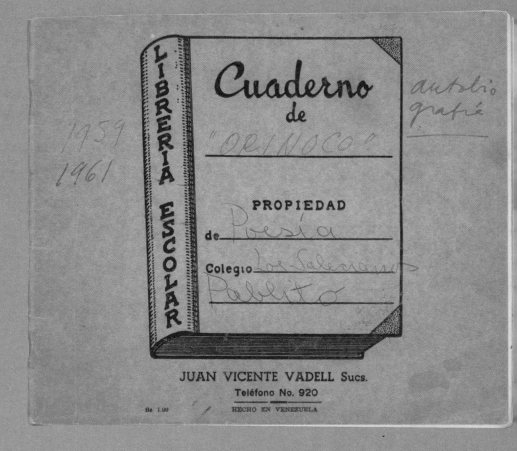

LIBRERÍA ESCOLAR

1959
1961

autobio
grafía

Cuaderno
de
"ORINOCO"

PROPIEDAD

de _Poesía_

Colegio _Los Salesianos_

Pablito

JUAN VICENTE VADELL Sucs.
Teléfono No. 920

Bs 1.00   HECHO EN VENEZUELA

THEN COME BACK
THE LOST NERUDA POEMS

TRANSLATED BY FORREST GANDER

COPPER CANYON PRESS
PORT TOWNSEND, WASHINGTON

Cover art: Photo by Sam Falk/New York Times Co./Getty Images

Forrest Gander's deep personal thanks to Kristin Dykstra, Julie Lynd, Edmundo Garrido, Anna Deeny, Raúl Zurita, and Valerie Mejer Caso.

Copper Canyon Press is in residence at Fort Worden State Park in Port Townsend, Washington, under the auspices of Centrum. Centrum is a gathering place for artists and creative thinkers from around the world, students of all ages and backgrounds, and audiences seeking extraordinary cultural enrichment.

LIBRARY OF CONGRESS CATALOGING-IN-PUBLICATION DATA

Names: Neruda, Pablo, 1904–1973, author. | Gander, Forrest, 1956– translator.
Title: Then come back : the lost Neruda Poems / Pablo Neruda ; translated by Forrest Gander.
Description: Port Townsend : Copper Canyon Press, 2016.
Identifiers: LCCN 2015048546 | ISBN 9781556594946 (hardback)
Subjects: LCSH: Neruda, Pablo, 1904–1973--Translations into English. | BISAC:
POETRY / Caribbean & Latin American.
Classification: LCC PQ8097.N4 A2 2016 | DDC 861/.62—dc23
LC record available at http://lccn.loc.gov/2015048546

98765432 FIRST PRINTING

Copper Canyon Press
Post Office Box 271
Port Townsend, Washington 98368
www.coppercanyonpress.org

CONTENTS

Temas

ausencia   anillo

loca mía mía   collar

                            aguja

            odas: perro   puma
                    caballo
                    canario
                    gato

        ojo!   corregir   verso en
                          el tiempo
                          que canta

PROLOGUE

IT'S TRUE, I've been caught in print several times saying, "The last thing we need is another Neruda translation." It's not that I don't love Pablo Neruda—I've translated his poems before—but given the attention he's justly received I've wanted to champion terrific lesser-known and more contemporary Latin American writers in translation. After all, a lot has happened *since* Neruda. For starters, Nicanor Parra, Raúl Zurita, Héctor Viel Temperley, Idea Vilariño, Alejandra Pizarnik, Antonio Cisneros, Coral Bracho, and now a new generation of hotshots.

So when I read, in late 2014, that never-before-seen poems by Neruda had been discovered, I initially shrugged it off. Not having read the poems, I assumed that someone was squeezing the last purple juices from the Neruda estate. Surely, I thought, the new poems were drafts, scraps, notes he hid away and never intended to publish. But then came the reviews in Spain and Latin America—and they were surprisingly, alarmingly enthusiastic.

When Copper Canyon Press asked me to consider translating the poems, I thought about what I'd need to give up to focus on a job like this. What do I ever give up to take on a translation project? My own writing goes on hold, but when, eventually, I come back to it, I bring to it something new—a feral vocabulary I've adopted from the translation, a fresh set of syntactical and rhythmical strategies, the image repertoire of someone else's imagination. I always come back from translation changed.

At this same moment and quite apart from the literary world, my mother was losing her faculties to Alzheimer's, and I was flying to Virginia every three weeks to spend time with her. My sister and I were in charge of all the stuff we had no idea how to manage: clearing the house of everything that constitutes the material of a long life— birding journals, decoys carved by Cigar Daisey, boxes of fossils, the Lionel train that puffed around our tree at Christmas—the very kinds of things that Neruda celebrated in his odes. We were tracking down deeds and wills and tax documents, frantically seeking help from lawyers and realtors as we tried to come to grips with what remained from a vibrant existence— and in this work, we shared, perhaps, dilemmas and uncertainties faced by those who discovered Neruda's lost poems.

So change—as in, "I always come back from translation changed"—sounded good to me. I was ready for some changes. Ready for these poems.

The manuscript Copper Canyon received was locked up like the Queen's jewels, so that I couldn't copy any part of it, couldn't print it, couldn't successfully email it to anyone else. For our book's presentation, Copper Canyon's editors and I have largely followed the lead of the original Spanish-language edition, as published by Seix Barral. However, in the introduction to that edition, the archivists and scholars expressed bafflement at lines that, perhaps due to my ignorance, didn't seem to me so hermetic. Their work, like my own, involved following traces and developing hunches, at times uncertain of the provenance of their discoveries. To cite an example, they were troubled by the phrase "es un movimiento florido de un siclo de sombra en el mundo," noting that their "initial impulse" was to read *siclo*—our word is the obsolete sicle or shekel, an ancient coin—as a typographical error for *siglo,* meaning century. They lugged in philology, Latin axioms, and a phrase by Juan Ramón Jiménez to help. But the Neruda line—which I came to render in English as "is but one florid flip of a blurry coin in the world"—made perfect sense to me in context.

Once I moved through the introductory material and into the poems, it was all over. Until then, I'd been reading the manuscript on my computer in a barn flanked on two sides by cemetery. When the glowing screen revealed the lost poems, hours suddenly clipped by in minutes. I neglected to come in for dinner. The windows opaqued with night. The world hushed as I translated the first three poems. The truth is that I disappeared from myself. I was concentrated entirely into the durable moment of translation—which begins in humility, a sublimation of the self so extreme that the music of someone else's mind might be heard. And for a while, no remnant of me existed outside of that moment.

I don't want to spoil the poems by talking too much about them here. There's a love poem that turned my solar plexus into a cavern. There's an ode to Neruda's wife's ear that depends upon a conceit that most Chileans today wouldn't fathom, since few remember the 1950s vernacular for abalone: "little ears of the sea." There's a poem in which Neruda recalls his arrival to Santiago at the age of seventeen. He'd come to cut his teeth on big-city poetry, but when he stepped off the train, he walked into squadrons of mounted police swinging batons at pro-testers in a widespread violence organized by the ruling elite, the nitrate barons, in a period that came to be called the White Terror. There are inclusive Whitmanesque paeans to laborers and there's a hilarious tirade against the depredations of the telephone. Neruda writes a kind of admonitory Rilkean letter to a young poet—to himself as a young poet. He addresses, in one of the most pro-found poems, the cosmos, Earth, and the first astronauts.

Not all of the poems are entirely finished. Some are handwritten on the backs of menus, some end in com-mas, some are typed up and corrected in Neruda's hand. Movingly, this edition includes holographic reproduc-tions: you'll see Neruda's handwriting, his cross-outs, his revisions. As when I first opened the lush facsimile edition of Emily Dickinson's folded letter-poems, I found this record of the working mind of a great poet riveting. All the more so because these poems were truly lost among the many boxes and files of Neruda's materials, rediscov-ered by Matilde Urrutia, Neruda's widow, when she and the archives director of the Neruda Foundation made a full inventory of their holdings.

There are some poems so emotively forceful, I have trouble reading them aloud without my voice cracking.

But instead of forecasting those, it might be fun here to consider a single poem, the oddest in the collection, the one that gave the Spanish-language editors fits. A typed version of this poem, dated June 1968, was found in a filing cabinet with some conference papers. Subsequently, a handwritten version turned up.

In my translation it begins: "Roa Lynn and Patrick Morgan / were moored in these waters." In the next lines, Lynn and Morgan sail off "to sea or to hell" while the dark river bearing "grief and blubbering" and all the particulars of our tumultuous world rushes toward us carrying—what else is it carrying? Something remarkable, we gather from the last lines. For the editors of the Spanish edition, this is an apocalyptic poem and the names Roa Lynn and Patrick Morgan refer to two of the ship figureheads that Neruda collected and fondly nicknamed *Jenny Lind* and *Henry Morgan*. How Jenny Lind became Roa Lynn and why the famous pirate captain Henry Morgan became Patrick remain unexplained. But to make matters a little less clear, the scholars add a series of curious etymological details, starting with the information that *roa*, in some language, may be a nautical term for the prow of a ship.

Two marvelous interventions solve the riddle of the poem for us. First, a Mexican journalist and reviewer of the Spanish edition of these lost poems bothered to google the perplexing names Roa Lynn and Patrick Morgan. He discovered both names in a May 1968 Argentine weekly. Here's my translation of the full newspaper notice:

POETS. Unintentionally but notably, the Buenos Aires Herald recently acted as matchmaker: an interview published two weeks ago has culminated in a marriage. When Patrick Morgan read, on April 13, the tale told by North American poet Roa Lynn Lanou, who spoke of herself, her country and the Brazilian favela where she lived for a while, Morgan asked his secretary to find her phone number. "I'm going to marry that girl, I said to my secretary," Morgan, sales manager for Brassovora and an occasional versifier, remembers saying. "My secretary answered I must be crazy." But that wasn't the case, clearly. On Tuesday, the 16th, Patrick and Roa met each other in the Golf Club in Palermo; after lunch, they read her poems and "spent the afternoon reciting Shakespeare." On Friday the 19th, the day Roa was supposed to leave for Chile, the lovers took off to Montevideo where they were married. On Monday, the 22nd, Roa moved into her new residence, a house in the North Barrio of the capital. On Tuesday, she rushed a cable of 30 words to her parents in Ohio, telling them the news.

The second intervention? I ran into Roa Lynn in New York. She has her own version of the events and she has her own copy of the poem, presented to her by Neruda himself. But that's her story to tell.

Meanwhile, Neruda offers something quite beautiful to us: this long-delayed gift.

FORREST GANDER

INTRODUCTION

IN 1986 THE PABLO NERUDA FOUNDATION assumed responsibility for the maintenance and preservation of the poet's estate, which includes a substantial collection of his typed and handwritten manuscripts. The documents in this collection are stored in cases specially designed for the preservation of paper, installed in a climate-controlled, armored vault. All the appropriate security measures are in place.

These poems, unpublished until now, escaped notice during an initial investigation by the poet's widow, Matilde Urrutia, who was first to organize the collection and to undertake the search for texts that were unpublished or had appeared only in hard-to-find journals. In spite of the care with which Matilde approached this work, some poems remained unpublished.

In June 2011 the Pablo Neruda Foundation set out to produce a catalogue as complete as possible of the poet's handwritten and typed manuscripts, describing the original documents at length, identifying which book each one belonged to, checking to see whether the texts were complete or fragmented, and comparing them with their published counterparts. This work required the inspection of every document in the collection, and along the way there were quite a few surprises.

It was an extraordinary journey to the interior of Neruda's poetry, in all its primordial materiality, because to work with the originals was to make contact with what we might call the poet's pulse. To see those first drafts was to return to the initial moment of each poem's creation. In his book *Maremoto*, Neruda describes the organisms and debris the sea deposits gradually onto the sand. Studying his manuscripts, at times we had the sense that waves of verse had washed over the paper and withdrawn, carrying with them revisions and reconsiderations, leaving the freshest version of each poem.

The inspection of the handwritten drafts, likely the first versions of many of the poems, was especially exciting. In them, the lines have a certain upward or downward slant. Occasionally they are broken by pen strokes crossing out or correcting words.

We noticed other details as well, like the kinds of writing materials the poet worked with: school notebooks from the fifties and sixties; loose sheets of paper; tablets of different sizes, some with unusual marks from other countries; university notebooks; various colors of ink. Sometimes Neruda wrote on the menus or musical programs of ships he was traveling on, his lines taking shape between appetizers, main courses, wines, and desserts.

Occasionally the typed versions, too, are flecked with handwritten edits. Then there are poems already polished or with minimal interventions. In this way—following the path of the poet's own hand, the ink ribbon, the typescript, or the carbon copy—the printed versions came to be.

Some poems, however, seemed to refuse the normative route. They were the minority, but that made them all the more compelling. There was no mark or indication to signal their exceptional unpublished status. We looked again and again, expecting to find traces of them in one of Neruda's many books or in the innumerable anthologies, but with no luck. It was as if the poems had hidden themselves in the jungle of the poet's manuscripts, camouflaged among thousands of sheets of paper and hundreds of thousands of words, in order to remain fugitive, unconquered.

These poems, never before seen, belong to a long period that spans from the beginning of the fifties to shortly before the poet's death in 1973. The process of transcription has been faithful to the poet's writing. Apart from adding diacritics in cases in which there was no ambiguity, the original orthography has been preserved, in particular with regard to the absence of punctuation marks. This facsimile edition includes some of the handwritten poems and provides a small sample of the variety of materials on which they were written. The notes that close the book reveal the particularities of each of the found manuscripts, offering keys to their dating and location within Neruda's body of work. It's important to point out that these are not variations of poems that have already been published but poems with their own lives, all of them situated within the great themes of Neruda's poetry: love, the landscape of his homeland, the world and the things that fill it, his own biography, journeys, the role of the poet, human responsibilities, and representations of the self.

For their literary quality and universal importance, there is no doubt that these poems deserve to be included among Pablo Neruda's published works. It is my belief that their appearance is a testament to the inexhaustible nature of this poet—inexhaustible not so much because these unpublished texts have been discovered, although that in itself is rare and constitutes a literary event of the first order, but because they allow for renewed readings, for numerous and varied reinterpretations of Neruda's vast body of work.

DARÍO OSES
LIBRARY AND ARCHIVES DIRECTOR
PABLO NERUDA FOUNDATION

TRANSLATED BY LIZZIE DAVIS

A Bordo del
"Usodimare"
partió el del
3 de Enero 1959
de Valparaíso.
Vamos a
Venezuela.
Artritis en los
dos tobillos!

THEN COME BACK

1

I touch your feet in the shade, your hands in the light,

and on the flight your peregrine eyes guide me

Matilde, with kisses your mouth taught me

my lips came to know fire.

Oh legs bequeathed the creaminess of perfect

oats, the battle spread,

its heart a meadow,

when I pressed my ears to your breasts,

my blood pounded out your Araucan syllable.

2

Never alone, with you

over the earth,

crossing through fire.

Never alone.

With you through the forests

finding again

dawn's

stiff arrow,

the tender moss

of spring.

With you

in my struggle,

not the one I chose

but

the only one.

With you through the streets

and sand, with you

my love, my exhaustion,

the bread, the wine,

poverty and glint of one coin,

wounds, sorrow,

happiness.

All the light, shadow,

stars,

all the cut wheat,

the corollas

of giant sunflowers, defeated

by their very fullness, the cormorant's

flight nailed

to the sky

like a coastline cross,

all

the space, the autumn, the carnations,

never alone, with you.

Never alone, with you, earth.

With you, the sea, my life,

all I am, all I give and everything I sing,

the substance of this

                         love, the earth

the sea,

bread, a life,

3

Where did you go What have you done

Ay my love

when not you but only your shadow

came through that door,

the day

wearing down, all

that isn't you,

I went searching for you

in every corner

imagining you might be

locked in the clock, that maybe

you'd slipped into the mirror,

that you folded your ditzy laugh

and left

it

to spring out

from behind an ashtray—

you weren't around, not your laugh

or your hair

or your quick footsteps

coming running

4

What guides autumn's singing leaf into your golden hand

or are you flinging ashes into the eyes of heaven

or did the apple offer you its scented light

or did you collude with a wave to choose the ocean's color?

It's been rain's right to adjust the stuff

of tears, to fall and rise, to tutor a biting silence

with spears that time and wind unfurl into leaves and smells

and it's clear the exuberant day sprinting by with its wagon
     of wheat

is but one florid flip of a blurry coin in the world

and I wonder if you don't work smithing the secret tin

for that white ship that skims our nocturnal night

or if a bead of your blood hasn't birthed the color of peaches

if it isn't your deep hands that make rivers run

if your eyes, wide-open to the hub of summer's sky,

don't make the sun drop its yellow sword earthward.

And then its ray strays over the rim of your glass, inciting

sand, corollas, volcanoes, jasmine, deserts, roots—

and it wafts your essence to the forest's eggs, to the furious
rose

of bumblebees, wasps, lions, snakes, falcons

that bite, sting, pierce, and brutalize your eyes weeping

because it was your seed in the soil, your impulsive ovary

that unleashed the sun's raving tongue over the earth.

Settle your perfect hips here and the bow of wet arrows

loosens into the night the petals that form your form

let your clay limbs climb the silence and its pale ladder

rung by rung taking off with me in my dream.

I can sense you scaling the shade tree that sings to the
shadows.

Dark is the world's night without you my love,

and I hardly recognize the source, barely make out the
language,

I strain even to decipher the eucalyptus leaves.

So if you stretch out your body, suddenly in the lugubrious
shadow,

your blood upwells into the river of time and I hear

the whole sky cascading through my love

and you're part of the wildfire that sparks my whole lineage, grant me then, by your golden life, the branch I've needed,

the flower that directs and sustains us,

the wheat that dies into bread and portions out our lives,

the mud with the smoothest fingers in the world,

the trains that whistle through frenzied cities,

the cluster of wallflowers, the weight of gold inside the earth,

the froth born and dying behind the boat and the wing

of a seabird rocking between waves like a clapper in a bell.

I cast my narrowing gaze across that awful country

where volcanoes were the natal fire, an agony,

where jungles burned to cinders of pumas and birds,

and you, my friend, could be the smoke's daughter,

you who may not have known you were born of fire and rage,

lightning over flaming lava etched your violet mouth,

your sex in the scorched oak's moss like a ring in a nest,

your fingers there in the flames, your compact body

rose from leaves of fire that make me recall

there were bakers in your family tree,

you're still the rainforest's bread, ash from violent wheat.

O love, from death to life one leaf from the forest, another
    leaf,

the proud foliage molders on the ground, the palace

of air and birdsong, the sumptuous house done-up in green

rots in shadow, in the water, in the chill.

We know that there, in moist decay, delicate seeds took root,

so the acacia lifts its perfume into the world again.

My love, my secret, my hard-bodied dove, my branch of
    nights, my star of sand,

the sanctuary of your wild-rose roots

soothes my soul's wars, those bright, high bonfires burning,

and I push through jungle, surrounded by crippled
    elephants,

a clamor of drums resounds in the rain, demanding my
    voice

and I make my way, my steps in step with my delirium

until your tower and cupola come into view

and I find, holding out my hand, your feral eyes

which were fixed on my dream and the stump of all my
    afflictions.

The thin hour waxed as the thin moon waxes in its sky,

it grew swollen cruising the air unhurried, unmarked

and we didn't imagine that you and I made up one element
of its motion,

that it's not merely hair, languages, arteries, ears that
compose the shadow of a man

but also a thread, a fiber stronger than nothing and no one,

our time coming and running down and swelling to fit this
attenuated hour.

Searching for the walls of Angol by dewlight in the fog,

we presumed they'd fallen, but devoured by war

a bulwark of sturdy wood remained, and liminal in the
moribund light,

the shadow or trace or dust of a burnt bone.

The forests of the sleepy South draped with vines,

the war and peace of the dead, anger and cold blood.

Sixty-four years this century drags along and sixty

of them this year are mine, now

whose eyes stare into the dead numbers?

Who are you, friend, enemy of my errant peace?

You know how the days went, the chronicle,

the revolutions, the trips, the wars,

the sicknesses, the deluges, the time that could seem like a
    routed soldier,

how shoes wore out racing through the offices of autumn,

what the men were doing in a mine, on the silvery heights of
    Chuquicamata

or on infinite Chile's Antarctic sea inside a ship shrouded in
    snow.

No matter, my ancient ways will keep teaching and singing
    to you

of what's bitter and electric in this impure, this radiant time
    with its

hyena fangs, atomic shirts, and wings of lightning,

for you with eyes yet to be born

I'll open pages of iron and dew to a blasted and blessed
    century,

a century gone brown as dark-colored men with tormented
    mouths

who, in my lifetime, came into a conscience and decent
    plumbing,

and came to claim a flag stained by centuries of blood and
    torture.

5

Crossing the sky I near

the red ray of your hair.

Of earth and wheat I am and as I close in

your fire kindles itself

inside me and the rocks

and flour ignite.

That's why my heart

expands and rises

into bread for your mouth to devour,

and my blood is wine poured for you.

You and I are the land full of fruit.

Bread, fire, blood, and wine

make up the earthly love that sears us.

Ministerio de Educación. Ley Nº 11.766

~~Donde fuiste~~ Qué has hecho
Ay amor mío
cuando por esa puerta
no entraste tú sino la sombra,
el día
que se gastaba, el aire todo
~~semimortuorio~~
lo que tú no eres,
fui buscándote
a todos los rincones,
me parecía
que en el reloj estabas, quizá
te escondiste en el espejo
que plegaste tu loca risa
y la
dejaste ~~dentro~~.
~~entre dos páginas~~
para que saltara
detrás de un cenicero.
no estabas, ni tu risa
ni tu pelo

vi tus pisadas rápidas
que corren
det

6

My heart, sun

of my poverty,

this is the day,

right?

this day,

it passed nearly forgotten

between one night

and the next,

between the sun and the moon,

welcome tasks

and work,

it passed nearly

snatched away

by the current,

transparent,

it nearly shot across

the water

but then

you plucked it up

with your hand

a fish

fresh

from the sky,

a huge drop of freshness,

brimming

with living fragrance

and moistened

by that

morning bell

like the tremor

of clover

at dawn,

and so

it passed into my hands

and made itself

your flag

and mine,

I remember,

and we rushed

through various streets

to find

bread,

dazzling

bottles,

a piece

of turkey,

some lemons,

one

branch

in bloom

as on

that

flowery

day

when

from the ship,

encircled

by the dark

blue of a sacred sea,

your tiny

feet brought you

descending

step by step

to my heart,

and the bread, the flowers

the stand-up

choir

of noon,

a sea wasp

over the orange blossoms,

all of that,

the pristine

light no

storm ever

switched off in our home,

came again,

surged and lived once more,

its freshness

swallowing the almanac.

Praised be the day

and that one.

Praised be

this

and every day.

The sea

will rock its bell tower.

The sun is a loaf of gold.

And the world whoops it up.

Love, there's no end to our wine.

7

Even in these steep

years

with a clear view of

the mountain range of my life

after having

climbed

the vertical snow

and reached

the diaphanous plateau

of unwavering light

I see you

near the snail-peddling sea

hoarding pinches

of sand

wasting time with

birds

that wing across

a marine loneliness

I look at you

and don't believe

I'm myself

so stupid, so remote,

so abandoned

A kid

just

arrived

from the provinces,

a poet

with trim eyebrows

and threadbare

shoes

you're

me

I who live

again,

just in from the rain,

your silence and your arms

are my own,

your verses

repetitious as

grains

of oats,

they have that tannic tang

of bird-and-leaf-carried

water from the forest

all right, young man, now

listen:

hang on

keep your silence

until the words

ripen

in you,

look at and caress

things

the hands

know, theirs is

a blind wisdom,

young man,

in life you'd better be

a good stoker,

an honest stoker,

don't presume

you'll be master of the pen,

an argonaut,

a swan,

a trapeze artist between high phrases

and the surrounding emptiness,

your obligation

is to coal and fire,

you must

dirty your hands

with burnt oil,

with smoke

from the cauldron,

wash yourself,

put on your new suit

and then

with heaven in reach you can

worry about the lily,

take on the orange blossom and the dove,

arrive into your radiance,

without forgetting the state

of oblivion,

of blackness,

without forgetting your own

or the earth,

toughen up

take a walk

over the sharp stones

then come back.

8

Lilac

leaves

all the leaves,

explosion

of foliage,

the earth's

trembling

canopy,

cypress that cleaves the air,

whispers of oak,

grass

borne by the wind,

emotive poplar groves,

leaves of eucalyptus

with the contours of

blood moons,

leaves,

lips and eyelids,

mouths, eyes, the hair

of the earth,

in the sand

barely

a drop

falls,

treetops brimming

with birdsong,

black chestnut,

last

to summon

sap and hoist it up,

magnolias and pines,

intense scents,

cool

apple trees shivering,

9

"Don't be vain," someone had scrawled

on my wall.

I don't recognize

the script or hand of

whoever left that line

in the kitchen. No one I invited, clearly.

He came in from the roof.

So who am I

supposed to answer? The wind.

Listen to me, wind.

For many years,

the vainest

have tossed in my face

their own empty vanities,

that is, they show me the door

I open at night, the book

I write,

the bed

that waits to receive me,

the house I build,

that is, that is, maliciously

they make signs with their fingers

entwined,

their viny fingers,

and all their self-love

they dump in my face,

they call me the things they are,

they bark at me their secrets.

Maybe

I'm vain,

I'm also vain.

Not about my poetry, I don't think.

Well, let's take a look.

All my life it's coursed through my body

like my own blood

which I decode

onto this paper, sometimes

I have work to do, they call me

and I don't come,

I'm given to write lines

I don't read,

I'm given to sing for someone

who one day

I'll never even meet.

It's true I get letters

that tell me:

your words

brought back my love,

they saved my life,

they reached me in prison,

and I think

that this circulating

blood, invisible blood

inside me

runs through other veins

from now on.

But as soon as

it leaves me,

I've forgotten my poetry.

There's no

serious

vanity in my forgetting

or in my creating,

nor

in my shoes

in my ancient

beat-up shoes,

bearing my vagrant feet,

every five years

I get myself a new suit,

my wilted

ties

don't exactly

gloat,

now

if at some time

when my people

are in danger

I check to see whether

our flag is still flying,

I race up

the bell towers

forgetting

the froth-

spitting wave,

forgetting

the flower

on the road,

I've done nothing

more than others,

maybe less than anyone,

Marvelous ear,

double

butterfly,

hear

your praise,

I'm not thinking

of abalone, "little

ears of the sea,"

most prized perhaps

of nacre's gifts,

kneaded

with rose flour,

no,

I want

to revere your ear

If they put

a boat

near a Chileno,

he jumps in,

he exiles himself

and is lost.

The rich man

heads to Vesuvius,

and won't face

the maternal

heights, the high

Andean flame,

he flies to Broadway,

to the Mayo Clinic,

to the Moulin Rouge,

the poor

Chileno, with his only

shoes

crosses into Neuquén, the

forsaken territories of Patagonia,

he hikes the lunary

shorelines of Peru,

he sets his hunger down

in Colombia,

migrates as he can,

changing stars like shirts,

the Chilena

is a crazy woman

with mutinous eyes,

an amiable heart, sky-blue skin

or he's the traveling salesman

with his wine, guitars,

water pipes

or he could be the sailor

who gets married

in Veracruz and never comes back

to his island,

to his fragrant oceanic Chiloé.

12

I rolled beneath hooves, the horses

passed over me like cyclones,

the moment clutched its flags,

and riding the student fervor

it blew into Chile—

sand and blood from niter quarries,

coal from backbreaking mines,

copper extracted into the snow

with our blood

and so the map was changing,

the pastoral nation bristled

into a forest of fists and horses,

and before I turned twenty I received,

amid the blows of police cudgels,

the throbbing

of a vast, subterranean heart

and in safeguarding others

I understood their lives were my own

and I came by friends

who will defend me to the last

because my poetry,

barely even shucked,

received the honor of their agonies.

13

Addled adolescence, sad and sweet,

quagmire of gloom

where leaves

and bodies tumble

with words,

hard blows and acid love,

an age like space,

rootless, open

and more unknown than the night,

dragging more stars than shadow.

Time rank with unreturned

touch,

with rocks under our feet and famished eyes,

with books life's lessons are squeezed from,

that—right over there—call us to notice though we don't,

with Baudelaire perched like a raven on a shoulder

and Lautréamont howling scot-free in his coffin.

In this manner,

far from Garcilaso and his riverbanks

festooned with swan feathers

and so half-cursed, the unhinged,

breast-fed on literature,

carrying every darkness in their hands,

derelict and delirious, go

trudging step by step,

taking to the road,

searching out bread, home, and woman

as all men must.

14

And the horses, where are they?

With so much living and dying,

well-schooled people

with their good-mornings spoken,

their clipped so-longs spoken,

didn't have time to say farewell

to their root-bound horses.

I rode a drop of rain

I rode a drop of water

but I was so little back then

I slid off the earth

and my saddle got lost

among horseshoes, low vines—

the man is too hard at work now

to glance into the thick forest

he no longer checks the leaves

nor do leaves fall from the sky for him

now the man is hard at work

hard at work digging his grave.

It's necessary to see how silence hangs

over the quake-rubbled outskirts of Valdivia

to know why the buried community

won't recognize the communion of roots

because those who fell dead there

died before dying.

And yet, as they say,

the heart is a leaf

and the wind makes it throb.

15

TO THE ANDES

Snow-pelted

cordilleras,

white

Andes,

walls

of my homeland,

so much

silence,

they hem in

the will, the struggles

of my people.

Above——the silvered

mountains,

below——the green thunder

of the ocean.

Still

these people

scratch at their bristling

lonelinesses,

they steer through

sheer waves

and in the afternoon

they find

a guitar,

and go for a walk singing.

My people

never hold back.

I know where they come from

and where

they'll go someday with that guitar.

That's why

I'm not unnerved

by the bloody sun hung out

over the whiteness,

the spectral cordillera

shutting down

the roads.

My people

toughened their hands

quarrying

jagged minerals,

they know

hard times,

and they go on,

they keep on.

We

Chilenos,

a poor people,

miners,

fishermen,

we want a taste

of what's happening

aside from the snow,

we scan the sea

for messages and news,

we're

holding on.

Come winter

the Andes

lay out

their infinite tablecloth,

Mount Aconcagua's

hoary mane

freezes to its white head,

the grand cordilleras

sleep,

the peaks

covered

with the same vast sheet,

the rivers

harden up,

all across the planet

snow keeps falling,

a multiplicity of shivers.

But

come spring,

death's mountains

are reborn,

the water's once again

a living substance, a song,

and a forgotten weed

pokes up,

later

everything is scented

with sweet mint or heady

araucarias,

beneath the mournful flight

of condors

the herons shoot out

from the silence.

Then

the whole cordillera

gives itself back

to the Chilenos,

and between the sea and the peaks

fires fan out.

Spring

swishes across the mountains

with its suit

of breezes,

yellow flowers

pour gold fragrance

into the earth's

old scars,

everything moving,

everything

in flight,

coming and going,

the news of the world,

the tendriling forth

of history, footsteps

of conquistadores overcome

by sheer labor,

and taller

than the highest rocks

is man,

at the crest

of the Andes

mankind,

the invincible

expansion,

the advance of the people.

And at the snow-covered

pinnacle,

lifting

his head, his hands

still holding a shovel,

the Chileno looks up

without fear, without sadness.

The snow, the sea, the sand

all of it is his road.

We'll keep up the fight.

16

Spring day,

a long Chilean day,

a long green lizard

lazing

on the amphitheater of snow

facing the navy blue.

Sun and water against

your green skin,

the resuscitated land

breathes behind your shield,

nodding off,

you lose your grip

but recover,

the pollen

stains you

red,

the cicadas

buzz by,

a bird

aims its bill at you,

you go on fully alive,

a fragrant
green creature
with a golden tail,

you give
and take sustenance,

you sing
and we sing of you,
sleepy
clear day
and you aren't even aware
that meantime
yellow beetles
are scrambling
up your head,
and violins
are taking wing
in your wind,
you don't know
who dies today,

you don't recognize

the mourners

trailing the cortege,

you don't know, can't conceive

of those evicted from their homes

last night, the woman

who lost her job,

the ring

slipping from the fingers

of the mother

as it clangs in the pawnbroker's drawer

like a lost cricket dying,

at ease

among so many

births,

the hub

of germinations,

attentive

in the wispy

spring of Chile,

you take it easy,

superb,

the sea's froth

like a sacred robe

nears and falls back

from your body,

and

the sky crowns you,

the ocean's chorus

etches into stone the song

of your praises,

among spiny thorns

of the cactus, the corolla burns,

the world is born again.

In the motherland of Chile

in spring

the voice,

the irregular theogony,

a bright abundance,

from green days lazing in the snow,

I draw out

this one day,

its face to the sea salt.

digo buenos días al cielo.
~~te cra~~
No hay tierra. Se desprendió
ayer y anoche del navío.
Se quedó atrás chile, solo,
unas cuantas aves salvajes
siguen volando, levantando
el nombre *oscuro* frío de mi patria.
Acostumbrado a los adioses
~~esta vez no te gastaron~~
no gasté los ojos: en donde
están encerradas las lágrimas?
La sangre subió de los pies
y recorre las galerías
del cuerpo pintando su fuego.
Pero donde se esconde el llanto?

52

Cuando llega el dolor acude.
Pero yo hablaba de otra cosa.
Me levante y sobre el navio
no había mas que cielo y cielo,
Cielo ~~de azul~~ azul interrumpido
~~por~~
una red de nubes tranquilas
inocentes como el olvido...
La nave es la nube del
Y he olvidé Cual es mi destino mar
olvidé la proa y la luna,
No sé hacia donde van las
ni donde me lleva la nave.
No tiene mar ni tiene el día.

X

17

I bid the sky good day.

There is no land. It slipped away

from the boat yesterday and last night.

Chile's been left behind, just

a few wild birds

follow us drifting and raising up

the dark cold name of my homeland.

Accustomed as I am to goodbyes

I didn't strain my eyes: where

are my tears bottled up?

Blood rises from my feet

and roves the galleries

of my body painting its flame.

But how do you stanch the moaning?

When it comes, heartache tags along.

But I was talking about something else.

I stood up and beyond the boat

saw nothing but sky and more sky,

blue ensnared in

a web of tranquil clouds

innocent as oblivion.

The boat is a cloud on the sea

and I've lost track of my destination,

I've forgotten prow and moon,

I don't remember where the waves go

or where the boat carries me.

There's no room in the day for earth or sea.

18

Comes back from his blaze, the fireman,

from his star the astronomer,

from his disastrous passion the obsessive,

from one million whatever the ambitious,

from the naval night the sailor,

the poet returns from his slabber,

the soldier from fear,

the fisherman from his wet heart,

the mother from Juanito's fever,

the thief from his nighttime high,

the engineer from his frosted rose,

the native from his hunger,

the judge from fatigue and unsureness,

the jealous from his torment,

the dancer from her exhausted feet,

the architect from the three thousandth floor,

the pharaoh from his tenth life,

the hooker from her Lycra and falsies,

the hero comes back from oblivion,

the poor from another day gone,

the surgeon from staring down death,

the fighter from his pathetic contract,

someone returns from geometry,

stepping back from his infinity, the explorer,

the cook from her dirty dishes,

the novelist from a web of lies,

the hunter stamps out the fire and returns,

the adulterer from rapture and despair,

the professor from a glass of wine,

the schemer from his backstabbing,

the gardener has shuttered his rose,

the bartender stoppers his liquor,

the convict takes up his plea again,

the butcher washed his hands,

the nun quit her prayers,

the miner his slick tunnel,

and like the rest I take off my clothes,

inside the night of all men, I make

a smaller night for myself,

my woman joins me, silence bears down

and the dream spins the world again.

19

Roa Lynn and Patrick Morgan

were moored in these waters,

bewildered on this river,

hostile, florid, morose,

they go off to sea or to hell,

with an intensifying love

that bathes them in light

or plucks them from the algea:

but the waters rush on

through darkness, full of voices,

a rhapsody of kisses and ashes,

streets bloodied by soldiers,

unacceptable reunions

of grief and blubbering:

so much carried by these waters!

our pace and place,

the ferment of the favelas

and ghoulish masks.

Just look what the water's carrying

up this four-armed river!

20

From isolation,

from the hostile bonehead I've always been

since even before I was born, between pride

and the terror of living without being loved,

I've come to shake hands with all the world

and, without wanting to at first, I've let myself

take phone calls, suffering

a voice, some advice through a wire,

a metallic transmission

until finally I took leave from myself

and raising my arms as though before

a pointed gun, I gave in

to the degradations of the telephone.

I who conducted myself with such singular tact

backing away from sterile offices,

from offensive industrial palaces

only to see some black apparatus

that even with its silence insults me,

me, a poet clumsy as a duck on land,

degrading myself to the point of yielding

my superior ear (which I consecrated

innocently to birds and music)

to this everyday prostitution,

affixing my ear to an enemy

trying to take control of my being.

I came to be a telefiend, a telephony,

a sacred telephant,

I prostrated myself whenever the ringing

of that horrid despot demanded

my attention, my ears and blood,

when a voice mistakenly

asked for technical information or an escort,

or it was a relative I detested,

a forgotten aunt, wholly objectionable,

a National Prize alcoholic

who longed to smack me

or a blue-tinged, syrupy actress

who wanted to violate me, seduce me

with her pink telephone.

I've changed clothes, roles,

I'm all ears,

I live trembling that they won't call me

or that they will, those idiots,

my anxiety is medicationproof,

doctors, priests, politicians,

maybe I'm turning myself into a telephone,

an abominable, black-lacquered instrument

through which others communicate

the contempt they'll devote to me

when I'm good for nothing

but the wasps that converse

across my body.

Those two solitary men,

those first men

up there,

what of ours did they

bring with them?

What from us, the men

of Earth?

It occurs to me

that the light was fresh then,

that an unwinking star

journeyed along

cutting short and linking

distances,

their faces unused

to the awesome desolation,

in pure space

among astral bodies polished and glistening

like grass at dawn,

something new came from the earth,

wings or bone-coldness,

enormous drops of water

or surprise

thoughts, a strange bird

throbbing

to the distant human heart.

And not only that,

but cities, smoke,

the roar of crowds,

bells and violins,

the feet of children leaving school,

all of that is alive

in space now,

from now on,

because the astronauts

didn't go by themselves,

they brought our earth,

the odors of moss and forest,

love, the crisscrossed limbs of men and women,

terrestrial rains over the prairies,

something floated up like

a wedding dress

behind the two spaceships:

it was our spring on earth

blooming for the first time

that conquered an inanimate heaven,

depositing in those altitudes

the seed

of our kind.

No hay tien

ayer y año

Se quedó a

unas cuanta

niguen volan

el nombre osc

A costumbre d

esta del no

no. gaste los

Se desprendió

del navío.

... chile, sólo

aves salvajes

y levantando

de una patria

... los adioses

... taron

... : en donde

1

Tus pies toco en la sombra, tus manos en la luz,

y en el vuelo me guían tus ojos aguilares

Matilde, con los besos que aprendí de tu boca

aprendieron mis labios a conocer el fuego.

Oh piernas heredadas de la absoluta avena

cereal, extendida la batalla

corazón de pradera,

cuando puse en tus senos mis orejas,

mi sangre * propagó tu sílaba araucana.

*Ilegible (N. del E.).

2

Nunca solo, contigo

por la tierra,

atravesando el fuego.

Nunca solo.

Contigo por los bosques

recogiendo

la flecha

entumecida

de la aurora,

el tierno musgo

de la primavera.

Contigo

en mi batalla,

no la que yo escogí

sino

la única,

Contigo por las calles

y la arena, contigo

el amor, el cansancio,

el pan, el vino,

la pobreza y el sol de una moneda,

las heridas, la pena,

la alegría.

Toda la luz, la sombra,

la estrellas,

todo el trigo cortado,

las corolas

del girasol gigante, doblegadas

por su propio caudal, el vuelo

del cormorán, clavado

al cielo

como cruz marina,

todo

el espacio, el otoño, los claveles,

nunca solo, contigo.

Nunca solo, contigo, tierra

Contigo el mar, la vida,

cuanto soy, cuanto doy y cuanto canto,

esta materia

                    amor, la tierra,

el mar,

el pan, la vida,

3

Donde fuiste Qué has hecho

Ay amor mío

cuando por esa puerta

no entraste tú sino la sombra,

el día

que se gastaba, todo

lo que no eres,

fui buscándote

a todos los rincones,

me parecía

que en el reloj estabas, que talvez

te escondiste en el espejo,

que plegaste tu loca risa

y la

dejaste

para que saltara

detrás de un cenicero

no estabas, ni tu risa

ni tu pelo

ni tus pisadas rápidas

que corren

4

Qué entrega a tu mano de oro la hoja de otoño que canta

o vas tú repartiendo ceniza en los ojos del cielo

o a ti te rindió la manzana su luz olorosa

o tú decidiste el color del océano en complicidad con la ola?

Ha sido la ley de la lluvia cambiar la sustancia

del llanto, caer y elevar, educar el amargo silencio

con lanzas que el viento y el tiempo transforman en hojas
      y aromas

y se sabe que el día entusiasta corriendo en su carro de trigo

es un movimiento florido de un siclo de sombra en el mundo

y yo me pregunto si tu no trabajas tejiendo el estaño secreto

del blanco navío que cruza la noche nocturna

o si de tu sangre minúscula no nace el color del durazno

si no son tus manos profundas las que hacen que fluyan los
      ríos

si no hacen tus ojos abiertos en medio del cielo en verano

que caiga del sol a la tierra su espada amarilla

Entonces recorre su rayo cruzando tu copa incitante

arenas, corolas, volcanes, jazmines, desiertos, raíces

y lleva tu esencia a los huevos del bosque, a la rosa
    furiosa

de los abejorros, avispas, leones, serpientes, halcones

y muerden y pican y clavan y rompen tus ojos llorando

pues fue tu semilla en la tierra, tu ovario impetuoso

el que repartió por la tierra la lengua del sol iracundo.

Reposa tu pura cadera y el arco de flechas mojadas

extiende en la noche los pétalos que forman tu forma

que suban tus piernas de arcilla el silencio y su clara
    escalera

peldaño a peldaño volando conmigo en el sueño

yo siento que asciendes entonces al árbol sombrío que
    canta en la sombra

Oscura es la noche del mundo sin ti amada mía,

y apenas diviso el origen, apenas comprendo el idioma,

con dificultades descifro las hojas de los eucaliptus.

Por eso si extiendes tu cuerpo y de pronto en la sombra
    sombría

asciende tu sangre en el río del tiempo y escucho

que pasa a través de mi amor la cascada del cielo

y que tú formas parte del fuego que corre escribiendo mi
    genealogía

me otorgue tu vida dorada la rama que necesitaba,

la flor que dirige las vidas y las continúa,

el trigo que muere en el pan y reparte la vida,

el barro que tiene los dedos más suaves del mundo,

los trenes que silban a través de ciudades salvajes,

el monto de los alhelíes, el peso del oro en la tierra,

la espuma que sigue al navío naciendo y muriendo y el ala

del ave marina que vuela en la ola como en un campanario.

Yo paso mi angosta mirada por el territorio terrible

de aquellos volcanes que fueron el fuego natal, la agonía,

las selvas que ardieron hasta las pavesas con pumas y
         pájaros,

y tú, compañera, talvez eres hija del humo,

talvez no sabías que vienes del parto del fuego y la furia

la lava encendida formó con relámpagos tu boca morada,

tu sexo en el musgo del roble quemado como una sortija en
         un nido

tus dedos allí entre las llamas, tu cuerpo compacto

salió de las hojas del fuego y en eso recuerdo

que aún es posible observar tu remoto linaje de panadería,

aún eres pan de la selva, ceniza del trigo violento.

Oh amor, de la muerte a la vida una hoja del bosque, otra
hoja,

se pudre el follaje orgulloso en el suelo, el palacio

del aire y del trino, la casa suntuosa vestida de verde

decae en la sombra, en el agua, en el escalofrío.

Se sabe que allí germinaron en la podredumbre mojada

semillas sutiles y vuelve la acacia a elevar su perfume en el
mundo

Mi amor, mi escondida, mi dura paloma, mi ramo de noches,
mi estrella de arena,

la seguridad de tu estirpe de rosa bravía

acude a las guerras de mi alma quemando en la altura la clara
fogata

y marcho en la selva rodeado por los elefantes heridos,

resuena un clamor de tambores que llaman mi voz en la lluvia

y marcho, acompaso mis pasos a mi desvarío

hasta ese momento en que surge tu torre y tu cúpula

y encuentro extendiendo la mano tus ojos silvestres

que estaban mirando mi sueño y la cepa de aquellos
quebrantos.

La hora delgada creció como crece la luna delgada en su cielo

creció navegando en el aire sin prisa y sin mancha

y no supusimos que tú y yo formábamos parte de su
movimiento,

ni solo cabellos, idiomas, arterias, orejas componen la
sombra del hombre

sino como un hilo, una hebra más dura que nada y que
nadie

el tiempo subiendo y gastando y creciendo en la hora
delgada.

Buscando los muros de Angol a la luz del rocío en la niebla

supimos que ya no existían, quedó devorado en la guerra

el bastión de madera maciza y apenas surgía en la luz
moribunda

la sombra o la huella o el polvo de un hueso quemado.

Los bosques del Sur soñoliento cubrieron con enredaderas

la guerra y la paz de los muertos, la ira y la sangre remota

Sesenta y cuatro años arrastra este siglo y sesenta

en este año llevaban los míos, ahora

de quién son los ojos que miran los números muertos?

Quién eres amigo, enemigo de mi paz errante?

Sabes cómo fueron los días, la crónica,

las revoluciones, los viajes, las guerras,

las enfermedades, las inundaciones, el tiempo que a veces
      pareció un soldado vencido,

cómo se gastaron zapatos corriendo por las oficinas de otoño,

qué hacían los hombres dentro de una mina, en la altura
      plateada de Chuquicamata

o en el mar antártico de Chile infinito dentro de un navío
      cubierto de nieve

No importa, mis pasos antiguos te irán enseñando y cantando

lo amargo y eléctrico de este tiempo impuro y radioso que
      tuvo

colmillos de hiena, camisas atómicas y alas de relámpago,

para ti que tienes los ojos que aún no han nacido

abriré las páginas de hierro y rocío de un siglo maldito y
      bendito,

de un siglo moreno, con color de hombres oscuros y boca
      oprimida

que cuando viví comenzaron a tener conciencia y
      alcantarillado,

a tener bandera que fueron tiñendo los siglos a fuerza de
      sangre y suplicio.

5

Por el cielo me acerco

al rayo rojo de tu cabellera.

De tierra y trigo soy y al acercarme

tu fuego se prepara

dentro de mí y enciende

las piedras y la harina.

Por eso crece y sube

mi corazón haciéndose

pan para que tu boca lo devore,

y mi sangre es el vino que te aguarda.

Tú y yo somos la tierra con sus frutos.

Pan, fuego, sangre y vino

es el terrestre amor que nos abrasa.

6

Corazón mío, sol

de mi pobreza,

es este día,

sabes?

este día,

casi pasó olvidado

entre una noche

y otra,

entre el sol y la luna,

los alegres deberes

y el trabajo,

casi pasó

corriendo

en la corriente

casi cruzó

las aguas

transparente

y entonces

tú en tu mano

lo levantaste

fresco

pez

del cielo,

goterón de frescura,

lleno

de viviente fragancia

humedecido

por aquella

campana matutina

como el temblor

del trébol

en el alba,

así

pasó a mis manos

y se hizo

bandera

tuya

y mía,

recuerdo,

y recorrimos

otras calles

buscando

pan,

botellas

deslumbrantes,

un fragmento

de pavo,

unos limones,

una

rama

en flor

como

aquel

día

florido

cuando

del barco,

rodeada

por el oscuro

azul del mar sagrado

tus menudos

pies te trajeron

bajando

grada y grada

hasta mi corazón,

y el pan, las flores

el coro

vertical

del mediodía,

una abeja marina

sobre los azahares,

todo aquello,

la nueva

luz que ninguna

tempestad

apagó en nuestra morada

llegó de nuevo,

surgió y vivió de nuevo,

consumió

de frescura el almanaque.

Loado sea el día

y aquel día.

Loado sea

este

y todo día.

El mar

sacudirá su campanario.

El sol es un pan de oro.

Y está de fiesta el mundo.

Amor, inagotable es nuestro vino.

Aun en estos altos
años
en plena
Cordillera de mi vida
después de haber
salido
la nieve vertical
y haber entrado
en plena multitud
con entreabierto corazón   a plena
a plena   canto
en la diáfana meseta
de la luz decisiva
llegué a la puerta
era de noche y
yo venía cansado

te veo
junto al mar caracolero
recogiendo vestigios
de la arena
perdiendo el tiempo con
los pájaros
que cruzan
la soledad marina
te miro
y no lo creo

soy yo mismo
tan tonto, tan remoto,
tan desierto

Joven
recién
llegado
de provincia,
poeta
de cejas afiladas
y zapatos
raídos
eres,
yo
yo que de nuevo
vivo,
que llegado de la lluvia,
tu silencio y tus libros
son los míos

Tequendi
Rocamai

Angusto
te quede
No
tus versos   tienen esa
esa fecundidad / de las avenas
en la tierra mojada
pero
cuanto tienes
que callar
defendiendo
el germen puro
de tu poesía,
cuanto ~~tienes~~
tienes que hablar
solo
el grano
repetido
de la avena,
la fecunda ~~dulzura~~ frescura
del agua en que ~~cazan~~ navegan Y

hojas y aves del bosque,
bien muchacho, y ahora
escucha.
    conserva
alarga tu silencio
hasta que todo en ti
madure(n)
las palabras,
mira y toca
las cosas,
& las manos
se ~~b~~ ~~guedando~~
guardan
ciega saben, tienen
sabiduría ciega,

muchedumbre, hay que
hay que ser en la vida
buen fogonero,
honrado fogonero,
no te metas,
a presumir de pluma,
de argonauta,
de cisne,
de trapecista entre las frases altas
y el redondo vacío,
tu obligación
es de carbón y fuego,
tienes
que ensuciarte las manos
con aceite quemado,
con humo

de caldera,
levante,
poniente traje nuevo
y entonces,
capaz de cielo puedes
preocuparte del la paloma,
                  lirio
usar el azahar y la paloma,
llegar a ser radiante,
sin olvidar tu condición de negro,
de negro,
de olvidado,
de negro.
sin olvidar los tuyos

ni la tierra,

endurécete

anda

camina

por las piedras agudas

recoge

las espinas,

las bellas, las

y regresa.

7

Aun en estos altos

años

en plena

cordillera de mi vida

después de haber

subido

la nieve vertical

y haber entrado

en la diáfana meseta

de la luz decisiva

te veo

junto al mar caracolero

recogiendo vestigios

de la arena

perdiendo el tiempo con

los pájaros

que cruzan

la soledad marina

te miro

y no lo creo

soy yo mismo

tan tonto, tan remoto,

tan desierto

Joven

recién

llegado

de provincia,

poeta

de cejas afiladas

y zapatos

raídos

eres

yo

yo que de nuevo

vivo,

llegado de la lluvia,

tu silencio y tus brazos

son los míos

tus versos tienen

el grano

repetido

de la avena,

la fecunda frescura

del agua en que navegan

hojas y aves del bosque,

bien muchacho, y ahora

escucha

conserva

alarga tu silencio

hasta que en ti

maduren

las palabras,

mira y toca

las cosas,

las manos

saben, tienen

sabiduría ciega,

muchacho,

hay que ser en la vida

buen fogonero,

honrado fogonero

no te metas

a presumir de pluma,

de argonauta,

de cisne,

de trapecista entre las frases altas

y el redondo vacío,

tu obligación

es de carbón y fuego,

tienes

que ensuciarte las manos

con aceite quemado,

con humo

de caldera,

lavarte,

ponerte traje nuevo

y entonces

capaz de cielo puedes

preocuparte del lirio,

usar el azahar y la paloma,

llegar a ser radiante,

sin olvidar tu condición

de olvidado,

de negro,

sin olvidar los tuyos

ni la tierra,

endurécete

camina

por las piedras agudas

y regresa.

8

Hojas

de lila

todas las hojas,

multitud

del follaje,

pabellón

tembloroso

de la tierra,

ciprés que clava el aire,

rumores de la encina,

hierba

que trajo el viento,

sensibles alamedas,

hojas de eucaliptus

curvas como

lunas ensangrentadas,

hojas,

labios y párpados,

bocas, ojos, cabellos

de la tierra,

apenas

en la arena

cae

una gota

copas

del trino,

castaño negro,

último

en recoger

la savia y levantarla,

magnolios y pinares,

duros de aroma,

frescos

manzanos temblorosós,

"No te envanezcas," alguien dejó escrito
en mi pared.
Yo no conozco
la letra ni la mano
del que inscribió la frase
en la cocina. No lo invité tampoco.
Entró por el tejado.
A quién entonces
contestar? Al viento.
Escúchame, viento.
Desde hace muchos años
los vanidosos
me echan en cara
mis propias y vacías vanidades,
es es, muestran la puerta
que alzo de noche, el libro
que trabajo,

El lecho
que me acoge,
la casa que construyo,
esos y es, ese es, malignos
me muestran con sus dedos
enredados,
dedos de enredaderas,
y cuando ellos se adoran
me lo tiran en cara,
lo que
cuanto son me designan,
lo que ocultan me ladran.
Tal vez
soy vanidoso, ~~de otro modo~~.
También soy vanidoso.
No de mi ~~poesía~~, me parece.
~~nunca~~
A ver, examinemos.
Toda la vida circuló en mi cuerpo

como una sangre propia
que descifro
en el papel, a veces
tengo que hacer, me llaman
y no acudo,
debo escribir renglones
que no leo,
debo cantar para alguien
que ni siquiera
conoceré algún día.

Es verdad que recibo
cartas que me dicen,
~~de alguien~~
tu palabra
me devolvió el amor,
me dió la vida,
me encontró en las prisiones,
y yo pienso

Que esta circulatoria
sangre, invisible sangre
que contengo
en otras venas vive
desde ahora.
Pero apenas
salió de mí
olvidé mi poesía.
No encuentro
grave
vanidad en mi olvido
ni en mi hallazgo,   X
tampoco
en mis zapatos
en mis viejos
zapatos deformados
por mis pies vagabundos,
cada cinco años

me hago un nuevo traje,
~~si~~ mis corbatas
~~están~~ marchitas
no se jactan
de nada,
ahora
si en el momento
de peligro
para mi pueblo
busco
la bandera,
~~escondido~~
subo
a los campanarios
olvidando
la ola
bordada con espumas,
olvidando
la flor
en el camino

no hice
mas que ninguno,
talvez menos que todos,

9

«No te envanezcas», alguien dejó escrito

en mi pared.

Yo no conozco

la letra ni la mano

del que inscribió la frase

en la cocina. No lo invité tampoco.

Entró por el tejado.

A quién entonces

contestar? Al viento.

Escúchame, viento.

Desde hace muchos años

los vanidosos

me echan en cara

sus propias y vacías vanidades,

ese es, muestran la puerta

que abro de noche, el libro

que trabajo,

el lecho

que me acoge,

la casa que construyo,

ese es, ese es, malignos

me muestran con sus dedos

enredados,

dedos de enredaderas,

y cuanto ellos se adoran

me lo tiran en cara,

lo que son me designan,

lo que ocultan me ladran.

Talvez

soy vanidoso,

también soy vanidoso.

No de mi poesía, me parece.

A ver, examinemos.

Toda la vida circuló en mi cuerpo

como una sangre propia

que descifro

en el papel, a veces

tengo que hacer, me llaman

y no acudo,

debo escribir renglones

que no leo,

debo cantar para alguien

que ni siquiera

conoceré algún día.

Es verdad que recibo

cartas que me dicen;

tu palabra

me devolvió el amor,

me dio la vida,

me encontró en las prisiones,

y yo pienso

que esta circulatoria

sangre, invisible sangre

que contengo

en otras venas vive

desde ahora.

Pero apenas

salió de mí

olvidé mi poesía.

No encuentro

grave

vanidad en mi olvido

ni en mi hallazgo,

tampoco

en mis zapatos

en mis viejos

zapatos deformados

por mis pies vagabundos,

cada cinco años

me hago un nuevo traje,

mis corbatas

marchitas

no se jactan

de nada,

ahora

si en el momento

de peligro

para mi pueblo

busco

la bandera,

subo

a los campanarios

olvidando

la ola

bordada con espuma,

olvidando

la flor

en el camino

no hice

más que ninguno,

talvez menos que todos,

10

Maravillosa oreja,

doble

mariposa

escucha

tu alabanza,

yo no hablo

de la pequeña

oreja

mas amada

hecha talvez de nácar

amasado

con harina de rosa

no,

yo quiero

celebrar una oreja

11

Al chileno

le ponen

cerca

un barco

y salta,

se destierra,

se pierde.

El rico

va al Vesubio,

desconoce

las alturas

maternales, el alto

fuego andino,

vuela a Broadway,

a la Clínica Mayo,

al Moulin Rouge,

el pobre

chileno, con sus únicos

zapatos

atraviesa el Neuquén, los territorios

desamparados de la Patagonia,

recorre los lunarios

litorales

del Perú,

se instala con sus hambres

en Colombia,

transmigra como puede,

cambia de estrella como de camisa,

es

la loca chilena

de ojos amotinados,

de fácil corazón, de piel celeste

o el vendedor viajero

de vino, de guitarras,

de cachimbas

o bien el marinero

que se casa

en Veracruz y ya no vuelve

a su isla,

a su fragante Chiloé marino.

12

Rodé bajo los cascos, los caballos

pasaron sobre mí como ciclones,

el tiempo aquel tenía sus banderas,

y sobre la pasión estudiantil

llegaba sobre Chile

arena y sangre de las salitreras,

carbón de minas duras

cobre con sangre nuestra

arrancado a la nieve

y así cambiaba el mapa,

la pastoril nación se iba erizando

en un bosque de puños y caballos,

y antes de los 20 años recibí,

entre los palos de la policía,

el latido

de un vasto, subterráneo corazón

y al defender la vida de los otros

supe que era la mía

y adquirí compañeros

que me defenderán para siempre

porque mi poesía recibió,

apenas desgranada,

la condecoración de sus dolores.

13

Adolescencia turbia, triste y tierna,

tembladeral sombrío

en que caen las hojas

los cuerpos,

las palabras

los golpes duros y el amor amargo,

edad como el espacio,

sin raíces, abierta

y más desconocida que la noche

con más estrellas que su sombra.

Tiempo impuro de tacto

sin respuesta,

de piedras en los pies y ojos con hambre,

de libros estrujados para aprender la vida

que allí mismo nos llama mira y que no vemos

con Baudelaire encima del hombro como el cuervo

y Lautréamont aullando en su féretro impune

Así,

lejos de Garcilaso y sus riberas

peinadas por las plumas de los cisnes

y así semi malditos, desquiciados

amamantados en literatura

con todas las tinieblas en la mano,

irresponsables y bravíos, ir

poco a poco andando,

caminando el camino,

buscando el pan, la casa y la mujer

como todos los hombres.

14

Y los caballos dónde están?

De tanto vivir y morir

las personas bien educadas

de tanto decir buenos días,

decir adiós con parsimonia

no se despidieron a tiempo

de los vegetales caballos

Yo monté una gota de lluvia

yo monté una gota de agua

pero era tan pequeño entonces

que me resbalé de la tierra

y se me perdió la montura

entre herraduras, raíces

está ocupado el hombre ahora

y no mira el bosque profundo

ya no investiga en el follaje

ni le caen hojas del cielo

el hombre está ocupado ahora

ocupado en cavar su tumba.

Hay que ver lo que es el silencio

en las afueras de Valdivia

por eso no conocerá

la comunidad del subsuelo

la comunión de las raíces

porque estos muertos fallecidos

murieron antes de morir.

Sin embargo, según entiendo

el corazón es una hoja

el viento la hace palpitar

15

Cordilleras

nevadas,

Andes

blancos,

paredes

de mi patria,

cuánto

silencio,

rodea

la voluntad, las luchas

de mi pueblo.

Arriba las montañas

plateadas,

abajo el trueno verde

del océano.

Sin embargo

este pueblo

pica las erizadas

soledades,

navega

las verticales olas

y en la tarde

toma

su guitarra,

y canta caminando.

Nunca

se detuvo mi pueblo.

Yo sé de dónde viene

y dónde

llegará alguna vez con su guitarra.

Por eso

no me asusta

el sol sangriento sobre

la blancura,

la espectral cordillera

cerrando

los caminos.

Mi pueblo

se endureció las manos

excavando

ásperos minerales,

conoce

la dureza,

y sigue andando,

andando.

Nosotros

los chilenos,

pueblo pobre,

mineros,

pescadores,

queremos

conocer lo que pasa

más allá de la nieve,

y del mar esperamos

mensajes y noticias,

nosotros

esperamos.

En el invierno

los Andes

revisten

su mantel infinito,

el Aconcagua

cristalizó las crines

de su cabeza blanca,

duermen

las grandes cordilleras,

las cumbres

bajo

la misma extensa sábana,

los ríos

se endurecen,

sobre el planeta cae

la nieve

como multiplicado escalofrío.

Pero

en la primavera

los montes de la muerte

han renacido,

el agua vuelve a ser

materia viva, canto,

y una escondida hierba

resucita,

luego

todo es aroma

de suave menta o graves

araucarias,

bajo el vuelo enlutado

de los cóndores

las garzas se despiden

del silencio.

Entonces

toda la cordillera

vuelve a ser territorio

para los chilenos,

y entre el mar y la altura

se multiplica el fuego.

La primavera

cruza las montañas

con su traje

de viento

las flores amarillas

llenan de oro fragante

las viejas cicatrices

de la tierra,

todo camina,

todo

vuela,

y van y vienen

las noticias del mundo,

el crecimiento

de la historia, los pasos

de los conquistadores abrumados

por el trabajo humano,

más altas

que las más altas piedras

está el hombre,

en la cima

de los Andes

el hombre,

el invencible

desarrollo,

el paso de los pueblos.

Y a la altura

nevada,

levantando

la cabeza, dejando

las manos en la pala

mira el chileno,

sin miedo, sin tristeza.

La nieve, el mar, la arena,

todo será camino.

Lucharemos.

16

Día de primavera,

largo día de Chile,

largo lagarto verde

recostado

en el anfiteatro de la nieve

frente al azul marino.

El sol y el agua sobre

tu piel verde,

respira en tus escudos

la tierra rediviva,

acostado

resbalas

y revives,

te mancha

el polen

rojo,

te zumban

las cigarras,

te picotea

un pájaro,

vives,

fragante

animal verde,

cola de oro,

nutres

y te nutres,

cantas y te cantamos,

dormido

día claro

no sabes

mientras

por tu cabeza

suben escarabajos

amarillos,

y los violines

vuelan

en tu viento,

no sabes

quién muere hoy,

no conoces

a los deudos

que siguen el cortejo

no sabes, no conoces

al que desalojaron de su casa

anoche, a la muchacha

que perdió su trabajo,

el anillo

que cayó de los dedos

de la madre

y sonó en el cajón del prestamista

como un grillo perdido que agoniza,

recostado

entre tantos

nacimientos,

nave

de las germinaciones

detenida

en la delgada

primavera de Chile,

reposas,

deslumbrante,

la espuma

como un manto sagrado

se acerca y se desprende

de tu cuerpo,

y

el cielo te corona,

el coro del océano

labra en la piedra el canto

en tu alabanza,

arde entre las espadas espinosas

la corola del cactus,

nace otra ves el mundo.

En la tierra de Chile

en Primavera

la voz,

la irregular teogonía,

el claro crecimiento,

yo recojo

un día,

de un día verde recostado en nieve,

frente a la sal marina.

17

Digo buenos días al cielo.

No hay tierra. Se desprendió

ayer y anoche del navío.

Se quedó atrás Chile, solo

unas cuantas aves salvajes

siguen volando y levantando

el nombre oscuro frío de mi patria.

Acostumbrado a los adioses

no gasté los ojos: en dónde

están encerradas las lágrimas?

La sangre sube de los pies

y recorre las galerías

del cuerpo pintando su fuego.

Pero dónde se esconde el llanto?

Cuando llega el dolor acude.

Pero yo hablaba de otra cosa.

Me levanté y sobre el navío

no había más que cielo y cielo,

azul interrumpido por

una red de nubes tranquilas

inocentes como el olvido.

La nave es la nube del mar

y olvidé cuál es mi destino,

olvidé la proa y la luna,

no sé hacia dónde van las olas,

ni dónde me lleva la nave.

No tiene mar ni tierra el día.

18

Regresa de su fuego el fogonero,

de su estrella el astrónomo,

de su pasión funesta el hechizado,

del número millón el ambicioso,

de la noche naval el marinero,

el poeta regresa de la espuma,

el soldado del miedo,

el pescador del corazón mojado,

la madre de la fiebre de Juanito,

el ladrón de su vértice nocturno,

el ingeniero de su rosa fría,

el indio de sus hambres,

el juez de estar cansado y no saber,

el envidioso de sus sufrimientos,

la bailarina de sus pies cansados,

el arquitecto del piso tres mil,

el faraón de su décima vida,

la prostituta de su traje falso,

el héroe regresa del olvido,

el pobre de un solo día menos,

el cirujano de mirar la muerte,

el boxeador de su triste contrato,

alguien regresa de la geometría,

vuelve el explorador de su infinito,

la cocinera de los platos sucios,

el novelista de una red amarga,

el cazador apaga el fuego y vuelve,

la adúltera del cielo y la zozobra,

el profesor de una copa de vino,

el intrigante de su puñalada,

el jardinero ha cerrado su rosa,

el tabernero apaga sus licores,

el presidiario anuda su alegato,

el carnicero se lavó las manos,

la monja canceló sus oraciones,

el minero su túnel resbaloso,

y como todos ellos me desnudo,

hago en la noche de todos los hombres

una pequeña noche para mí,

se acerca mi mujer, se hace el silencio

y el sueño vuelve a dar la vuelta al mundo.

19

Roa Lynn y Patrick Morgan

en estas aguas amarrados,

en este río confundidos,

hostiles, floridos, amargos,

van hacia el mar o hacia el infierno,

con un amor acelerado

que los precipita en la luz

o los recoge del sargazo:

pero continúan las aguas

en la oscuridad, conversando,

contando besos y cenizas,

calles sangrientas de soldados,

inaceptables reuniones

de la miseria con el llanto:

cuanto pasa por estas aguas!:

la velocidad y el espacio,

los fermentos de las fabelas

y las máscaras del espanto.

Hay que ver lo que trae el agua

por el río de cuatro brazos!

20

Del incomunicado,

del ignorante hostil que yo fui siempre

desde antes de nacer, entre el orgullo

y el terror de vivir sin ser amado,

pasé a darle la mano a todo el mundo

y me dejé telefonear sin ganas

al principio, aceptando

una voz, un alámbrico consejo,

una metálica comunicación

hasta que ya me fui de mí yo mismo

y levantando como ante un revólver

los brazos, me entregué

a las degradaciones del teléfono.

Yo que me fui con tacto singular

alejando de claras oficinas,

de ofensivos palacios industriales

solo de ver un aparato negro

que aun silencioso me insultaba,

yo, poeta torpe como pato en tierra,

fui corrompiéndome hasta conceder

mi oreja superior (que consagré

con inocencia a pájaros y música)

a una prostitución de cada día,

enchufando al oído el enemigo

que se fue apoderando de mi ser.

Pasé a ser telefín, telefonino,

telefante sagrado,

me prosternaba cuando la espantosa

campanilla del déspota pedía

mi atención, mis orejas y mi sangre,

cuando una voz equivocadamente

preguntaba por técnicos o putas,

o era un pariente que yo detestaba

una tía olvidada, inaceptable,

un Premio Nacional alcoholista

que a toda costa quería pegarme

o una actriz tan azul y almibarada

que quería violarme, seducirme

empleando un teléfono rosado.

He cambiado de ropa, de costumbres,

soy solamente orejas,

vivo temblando de que no me llamen

o de que me llamen los idiotas,

mi ansiedad resistió medicamentos,

doctores, sacerdotes, estadistas,

talvez voy convirtiéndome en teléfono,

en instrumento abominable y negro

por donde comuniquen los demás

el desprecio que me consagrarán

cuando yo ya no sirva para nada

es decir para que hablen

a través de mi cuerpo las avispas.

21

Estos dos hombres solos,

estos primeros hombres

allá arriba

qué llevaron consigo

de nosotros?

De nosotros los hombres,

de la Tierra?

Se me ocurre

que aquella luz fue nueva,

aquella estrella aguda

que viajaba,

que tocaba y cortaba

las distancias,

aquellos rostros nuevos

en la gran soledad,

en el espacio puro

entre los astros finos y mojados

como la hierba en el amanecer,

algo nuevo venía de la tierra,

alas o escalofrío,

grandes gotas de agua

o pensamiento

imprevisto, ave extraña

que latía

con el distante corazón humano.

Pero no sólo aquello,

sino ciudades, humo,

ruido de multitudes,

campanas y violines,

pies de niños saliendo de la escuela,

todo eso en el espacio

vive ahora,

desde ahora,

porque los astronautas

no iban solos,

llevaban nuestra tierra,

olor de musgo y bosque,

amor, enlace de hombres y mujeres,

lluvia terrestre sobre la pradera,

algo flotaba como

un vestido de novia

detrás de las dos naves del espacio:

era la primavera de la tierra

que florecía por primera vez,

que conquistaba el cielo inanimado

dejando en las alturas

la semilla

del hombre.

Día 29 - Diciembre 1952
11 de la mañana
volando a 3.500 mts
de altura entre
Recife y Río Janeiro

MENU

Por el cielo me acerco
al rayo rojo de tu cabellera.
De tierra y trigo soy y al acercarme
tu fuego se prepara
dentro de mí y enciende
las piedras y la harina.
Por eso crece y sube
mi corazón haciéndose
pan para que tu boca lo devore.
Y mi sangre es el vino que te
                        aguarda.
Tú y yo somos la tierra con
                        sus frutos.
Pan, fuego, sangre y vino
es el terrestre amor que nos
                        abrasa.

NOTES

POEM 1

This poem, like many of Neruda's, is dedicated to Matilde Urrutia, his third wife and principal muse. It is written by hand on a single page, with many revisions. It was found in a notebook that also contains the original manuscript of *Memorial de Isla Negra* (Isla Negra memorial); two poems from *Plenos poderes* (Full powers): "Oda a Acario Contapos" (Ode to Acario Contapos) and "A don Asterio Alarcón, cronometrista de Valparaíso" (To Don Asterio Alarcón, timekeeper of Valparaíso); and a prose piece on Venezuela dated January 23, 1959. This poem, numbered 1, came immediately after the prose and can therefore be dated to between 1959 and sometime in 1960.

POEM 2

This poem was found in a notebook with "Odas" written on the front cover and "1956" on the first page. It's a continuation of Neruda's manuscript of odes tentatively titled "Naufragio de navío enlutado" (Sinking of a ship in mourning), published as "Oda al barco pesquero" (Ode to the fishing boat) in his *Tercer libro de las odas* (Third book of odes). The beginning of a draft of a poem very likely dedicated to Matilde follows: "No estás hecha de sueño, amor amado / Eres compacta como una manzana. / Repleta eres de luz, rosa rosaria / y al trasluz eres como uva agraria."[1]

These verses are crossed out. On the next page, there are additional lines in free verse, also rejected, and finally there is the

---

1.   "You are not made of dreams, beloved love / You are solid as an
     apple. / You are brimming with light, rosary rose / and held to the
     light you're like an agrarian grape."

first draft of "Oda al viejo poeta" (Ode to the old poet), also published in *Tercer libro de las odas*. It is likely, then, that "Never alone, with you" was written for this book in 1956, although it was ultimately not included.

POEM 3

This is the first of the poems in a notebook that also contains the manuscripts of "Al tiempo que me llama" (While you are calling me), published as "Oda al tiempo venidero" (Ode to coming times) and dated September 22, 1956; "Oda a unas flores amarillas" (Ode to some yellow flowers), dated the same day; and "Odas de todo el mundo" (Odes from all over the world), all of which come from *Tercer libro de las odas,* as well as "Oda al plato" (Ode to the plate) from *Navegaciones y regresos* (Voyages and homecomings). It was likely written around September 1956.

On the first page of the notebook Neruda has made some loose annotations: "Temas – Ausencia – Loca mía."[2] In another column: "odas: perro – caballo puma – canario – gato."[3] Finally: "ojo! – corregir – verso en – al tiempo – que canta."[4] These notes make reference, in part, to possible themes for odes. In fact, in *Navegaciones y regresos,* the poet includes odes to the dog, the horse, and the cat. The theme of absence could correspond to this very poem, "Where did you go What have you done."

---

2.   "Themes – Absence – My lunatic"

3.   "odes: dog – horse puma – canary – cat"

4.   "careful! – correct – in verse – while – it sings"

Judging by the lines "Sesenta y cuatro años arrastra este siglo y sesenta / en este año llevaban los míos,"[5] Neruda wrote this poem in 1964. That same year, at age sixty, he published his poetic autobiography, *Memorial de Isla Negra,* and wrote the first part of *La barcarola* (Barcarole).

"What guides autumn's singing leaf into your golden hand" has the makings of the love poems we find in *Memorial de Isla Negra,* the long lines and allusions to the rural origins of the beloved that can be found, for example, in "Tú entre los que parecían extraños" (You among those who seemed strange): "allí en los caminos abiertos por reinos después devorados, / hacías cantar tus caderas y te parecías, antigua y terrestre araucana."[6]

This poem also seems to anticipate *Fin del mundo* (*World's End*[7]), which Neruda began writing in 1968, especially when, for example, the poet speaks of "lo amargo y eléctrico de este tiempo impuro y radioso que tuvo / colmillos de hiena, camisas atómicas y alas de relámpago"[8] and of "las páginas de hierro y rocío de un siglo maldito y bendito."[9]

Only a typed version of this poem exists.

---

5. "Sixty-four years this century drags along and sixty / of them this year are mine"

6. "there on the paths opened by kingdoms later devoured, / you made your hips sing and you appeared, ancient and earthly, Araucanian"

7. Copper Canyon Press (2009), translated by William O'Daly.

8. "what's bitter and electric in this impure, this radiant time with its / hyena fangs, atomic shirts, and wings of lightning"

9. "pages of iron and dew to a blasted and blessed century"

POEM 5

This poem was handwritten on one page of a menu, kindly furnished for this book by Jorge Selume Zarzor. On it, a note has been made in what looks like Matilde's hand: "Día 29 – Diciembre 1952 – 11 de la mañana – volando a 3.500 metros – de altura entre – Recife y Río Janeiro."[10] Neruda may have written it on the return trip from Europe to Atlántida, Uruguay, where he joined Matilde to celebrate the New Year.

POEM 6

This poem, written on loose-leaf, was found in a box, most of the contents of which appeared in *Nuevas odas elementales* (New elemental odes) or *Navegaciones y regresos*. In it, Neruda writes: "tus menudos / pies te trajeron / bajando / grada y grada / hasta mi corazón."[11] We find similar references to Matilde's small feet throughout his work. In "La pasajera de Capri" (The passenger from Capri) from *Las uvas y el viento* (The grapes and the wind), for instance, he writes: "y estos menudos pies fueron midiendo / las volcánicas islas de mi patria."[12] Later, in "El amor" (Love) from *La barcarola*, he writes: "leí el alfabeto / que tus pies menudos dejaban andando en la arena."[13]

---

10. "29th day of December 1952 – 11 in the morning – flying at 3,500 meters – between – Recife and Río Janeiro"

11. "your tiny / feet brought you / descending / step by step / to my heart"

12. "and these tiny feet were measuring / the volcanic islands of my country"

13. "I read the alphabet / your tiny feet left walking in the sand"

POEM 7

In this particularly interesting poem, an experienced poet gives professional advice to the young poet he once was. The suggestions Neruda offers to his own youthful "I" can also be extended to other young poets. In part, what makes this poem notable is its singularity: to our knowledge, there's nothing in Neruda's body of work that resembles what *Letters to a Young Poet* was for Rainer Maria Rilke. Neruda tells the young poet "a presumir de pluma, / de argonauta, / de cisne, / de trapecista entre las frases altas / y el redondo vacío"[14] but instead to dirty his hands, to work with particulars and rudiments, with coal and fire. Here, he uses the image of poet-as-stoker to depict the poet as a man like any other—not marked for a superior destiny, not like Huidobro's "little god"—and his profession as one among many. At other moments in Neruda's work, including in his Nobel Prize acceptance speech, he employs the image of poet-as-baker, tenderly and diligently fulfilling a role as humble as it is necessary for the community.

This poem was discovered in a box that contains mainly manuscripts of odes (to spring, to Walt Whitman, to Louis Aragon) later included in various books: *Odas elementales* (Elemental odes), *Nuevas odas elementales,* and *Navegaciones y regresos.*

POEM 8

This poem, written on loose-leaf, belongs undoubtedly to Neruda's ode period. It is consistent with the poet's wish to, in the words of Saúl Yurkievich, expand the sphere of poetry "to

---

14. "don't presume / you'll be master of the pen, / an argonaut, / a swan, / a trapeze artist between high phrases / and the surrounding emptiness"

encompass the whole world, to fully embrace the scope of the real." To this end, each ode engages with its subject in the singular and unrepeatable moment in which the poet encounters it. "Oda a una castaña en el suelo" (Ode to a chestnut on the floor), for example, is not an ode to all chestnuts, but rather to a specific chestnut encountered at a unique and transitory point in time. "Lilac," in which the poet perceives a landscape of leaves that he fixes in his poetry just before the world is erased, seems to belong to this category of ode as well, as does "Oda a un ramo de violetas" (Ode to a violet bouquet).

This poem was also found in the box of manuscripts of odes later included in various books: *Odas elementales, Nuevas odas elementales,* and *Navigaciones y regresos.*

POEM 9

This poem, written on loose-leaf, was also found in the box of manuscripts of odes (to spring, to Walt Whitman, to Louis Aragon) that were later included in *Odas elementales, Nuevas odas elementales,* and *Navigaciones y regresos.* It bears a certain resemblance to "Oda a la envidia" (Ode to envy) from *Odas elementales,* in which the poet recounts his experiences with the envy of others: "Se irguieron / amenazantes / contra mi poesía, / con ganchos, con cuchillos, / con alicates negros."[15] Nevertheless, he proclaims that he must go on fulfilling his duties as poet: "Qué puedo hacer? / Yo creo / que seguiré cantando / hasta morirme";[16] "escribiré no sólo / para no morirme,

---

15. "They rose up / looming / against my poetry, / with hooks, with knives, / with black pliers"

16. "What can I do? / I think / I'll keep singing / until I die"

/ sino para ayudar / a que otros vivan, / porque parece que alguien / necesita mi canto."[17]

Neruda addresses the same invisible enemies in "Don't be vain," in which, singled out and condemned, he must continue to realize his role as poet and citizen. The idea that the poet should speak with the voice of the people or translate the collective life, further developed in other texts and drawn in part from Whitman, also surfaces here: "Toda la vida circuló en mi cuerpo / como una sangre propia / que descifro / en el papel."[18]

POEM 10

This poem may have been a first attempt at "Oda a la oreja" ("Ode to the ear"), left unfinished. Its most obvious poetic relations are the odes that Neruda wrote to various parts of the body: the skull, the liver, the eye. It was found in a box that contains mainly manuscripts of odes (to spring, to Walt Whitman, to Louis Aragon) that were later included in *Odas elementales, Nuevas odas elementales,* and *Navegaciones y regresos.*

POEM 11

This poem, written on loose-leaf, was discovered in a box that contains mainly manuscripts of odes (to spring, to Walt Whitman, to Louis Aragon) later included in *Odas elementales, Nuevas odas elementales,* and *Navegaciones y regresos.* It could be considered

---

17. "I'll write not just / to keep from dying, / but to help / others live, / because it seems like someone / needs my song"

18. "All my life it's coursed through my body / like my own blood / which I decode / onto this paper"

an ode to the Chileno traveler and would fit well in the last of the aforementioned books, if the six crossed-out lines that close the original manuscript are taken into account: "Chileno, no te vayas, / no te vayas, chileno. / Esta tierra / delgada / nos tocó / en la baraja turbulenta / del siglo xv y de la geografía."[19]

It's interesting that after establishing the condition of the Chileno traveler, often referred to in the country as *pata de perro* (dog foot, someone who, in U.S. parlance, "hoofs it"), Neruda entreats him not to abandon his homeland, and then he rejects those lines. Though discarded here, the idea is consistent with words from a speech the poet made on June 20, 1954, when he donated his collection of seashells and books to the University of Chile: "El poeta no es una piedra perdida. Tiene dos obligaciones sagradas: partir y regresar [...]. Sobre todo en estas patrias solitarias, aisladas entre las arrugas del planeta, testigos integrales de los primeros signos de nuestros pueblos, todos, todos, desde los más humildes hasta los más orgullosos, tenemos la fortuna de ir creando nuestra patria, de ser todos un poco padres de ella."[20] In this poem, the richest and most powerful travelers appear alongside the most modest, and, taking the crossed-out lines into consideration, all are equally driven to voyages and homecomings."

19. "Chileno, don't go / don't go, Chileno. / This slim / country / dealt us into / the turbulent deck / of the fifteenth century, of geography."

20. "The poet is not a lost pebble. He has two sacred obligations: to go and to come back.... Above all, in these solitary countries, isolated among the wrinkles of the planet, fundamental witnesses to the very first signs of our people, all of us, all of us, from the most humble to the most proud, have the fortune to go on creating our homeland, to all, in some way, however small, be her guardian"

POEM 12

This poem was found in a notebook that also contains the original manuscript of *Memorial de Isla Negra;* two poems from *Plenos poderes,* "Oda a Acario Cotapos" and "A don Asterio Alarcón, cronometrista de Valparaíso"; and a prose piece on Venezuela dated January 23, 1959. It comes immediately after a poem titled "La poesía II" (Poetry II), published in *Memorial de Isla Negra* as "Arte magnética" (Magnetic art) and dated April 24, 1961, and was written at eleven in the morning the following day. In it, Neruda alludes to Santiago, a city he visited for the first time at seventeen in 1921. He describes the social and political disorder of the early 1920s, during which the mounted police would often attack protesters. This image is the basis for the lines "Rodé bajo los cascos, los caballos / pasaron sobre mí como ciclones."[21]

In reference to this period, the poet notes in his memoir: "Los estudiantes apoyábamos las reivindicaciones populares y éramos apaleados por la policía en las calles de Santiago."[22]

This poem and the following one, "Addled adolescence, sad and sweet," dated April 26, 1961, and also written in Isla Negra, both refer clearly to the poet's youth; though they were ultimately not included, they must have been written for *Memorial de Isla Negra.*

POEM 13

This poem's location was indicated in the previous note. It remains to be added, however, that the antibookish position

---

21. "I rolled beneath hooves, the horses / passed over me like cyclones"

22. "We, the students, were supporting the demands of ordinary people, and we were beaten by the police on the streets of Santiago."

Neruda takes in various writings, in which literature is placed in opposition to life, appears here as well. It's a stance summed up in the first lines of "Oda al libro (I)" (Ode to the Book [I]): "Libro, cuando te cierro / abro la vida."[23] In "Addled adolescence, sad and sweet," there are references to some of the authors Neruda read: Baudelaire, Lautréamont, and Garcilaso. Two of the lines reference those who are "amamantados en literatura / con todas las tinieblas en la mano."[24] From such darkness, which appears to be brought on by bookishness and intellectualism, the poet moves little by little toward life, toward the common human experience: the search for "el pan, la casa y la mujer."[25]

POEM 14

This poem was found on the reverse sides of two musical programs from April 4 and 5, 1967, on the Italian Line's transatlantic *Augustus*. It was likely written during Neruda and Matilde's voyage aboard the ship, which began on March 31, 1967. The poem's central theme is the deaths of others, specifically those who "murieron antes de morir."[26] Based on the date on which "And the horses, where are they?" was likely written (several years after the devastating "Great Chilean Earthquake" that leveled the city of Valdivia), its dark tone, and its thematic content, we might look for poetic affinities in Neruda's collection *Las manos del día* (*The Hands of Day*[27]).

---

23. "Book, when I close you / I open life."

24. "breast-fed on literature, / carrying every darkness in their hands"

25. "bread, home, and woman"

26. "died before dying"

27. Copper Canyon Press (2008), translated by William O'Daly.

POEM 15, TO THE ANDES

This poem was written on April 26 at 12:30 p.m. in Los Guindos. While the year is not indicated, it was likely between 1952, when Neruda returned to Chile after his exile, and 1954, the last year he spent in Los Guindos. It undoubtedly belongs to the period during which he wrote his *Odas elementales*, bearing a clear resemblance to "Oda a la cordillera andina" (Ode to the Andes) from *Nuevas odas elementales*. In both poems, descriptions of the mountainous landscape alternate with exaltation of man's work. *Alturas de Macchu Picchu* (*The Heights of Macchu Picchu*[28]) explores a similar theme, and the mountain range and mineral work come up at other moments in Neruda's poetry: "El cobre" (Copper) and "La noche en Chuquicamata" (Night in Chuquicamata) from *Canto general*, "Oda al cobre" from *Odas elementales*, "La hermana cordillera" (The sister cordillera) from *Memorial de Isla Negra*, various poems titled "Volcán" (Volcano) in *La espada encendida* (The flaming sword), and others.

POEM 16

"Ode to a Spring Day" would make a suitable title for this poem, dated October 13, 1954, in Los Guindos; its focus is narrower than that of "Oda a la primavera," published in July 1952 in *Odas elementales*. Since "Día de primavera" came later, the poet must have written it with another book of odes in mind. Other poems in Neruda's body of work address the same theme: "Oda a las alas de septiembre" (Ode to the wings of September) from *Navegaciones y regresos* and "Primavera en Chile" (Spring in Chile) from *La barcarola*. "Spring day" was found in a box that contained, for the most part, poems included in two books of odes, *Navegaciones y regresos* and *Nuevas odas elementales*.

---

28. Copper Canyon Press (2015), translated by Tomás Morín.

POEM 17

This poem appears on the first two pages of a notebook that
contains the manuscript of the long poem "La insepulta de
Paita" (The unburied woman of Paita), published in *Cantos
ceremoniales* (Ceremonial songs). Although it can be read inde-
pendently, it's possible that "I bid the sky good day" was written
as a sort of prelude for "La insepulta de Paita," which tells the
story of a voyage to Venezuela during which the poet stopped
briefly in Paita. For whatever reason, the poem was replaced by
a prologue that describes the same journey:

> Desde Valparaíso por el mar.
> El Pacífico, duro camino de cuchillos.
> Sol que fallece, cielo que navega.
> Y el barco, insecto seco, sobre el agua.
> Cada día es un fuego, una corona.
> La noche apaga, esparce, disemina.
> Oh día, oh noche,
> oh naves
> de la sombra y la luz, naves gemelas!
> Oh tiempo, estela rota del navío!
> Lento, hacia Panamá, navega el aire.
> Oh mar, flor extendida del reposo!
> No vamos ni volvemos ni sabemos.
> Con los ojos cerrados existimos.[29]

---

29. "From Valparaiso by sea. / The Pacific, arduous path of knives.
    / The dying sun, the drifting sky. / And the ship, a dry insect over
    the water. / Every day is a flame, a crown. / Night is smothered: it
    thins out, it scatters. / Oh day, oh night, / oh ships / of shadow and
    light, twin vessels! / Oh time, broken wake of the ship! / Slowly,
    toward Panama, guided by air. / Oh sea, unfurled flower of stillness!
    / We do not go, or come back, or know. / Eyes closed, we exist."

On the first page of the notebook where the manuscript was found, Neruda writes: "A bordo del 'Uso di mare' partió el 3 de Enero 1959 de Valparaíso. Vamos a Venezuela. Artritis en los dos tobillos!"[30]

POEM 18

This poem is dated October 17, 1958. It was found in a notebook with "Odas elementales" written on its cover and "Al rey de bastos" (To the king of clubs) on the first page. Apart from this poem, the notebook contains exclusively odes (to the watermelon, to the elephant, to the bed, to the anchor, to the chair, and to the guitar), all of which can be found in *Navegaciones y regresos*. Although *Navegaciones y regresos* is considered Neruda's fourth book of elemental odes, it does include some poems that are not odes and seems to be one of the volumes in which the poet assembles diverse materials. "Comes back from his blaze, the fireman" could have been another of the book's outliers, but it was ultimately not included. As can be seen, the poem is constructed with a long list of professions as its foundation, each one connected with its requisite materials. In *The Hands of Day,* written ten years later, the poem "El llanto" ("The Weeping") is fashioned in a similar way:

> Dice además el hombre
> que odia su *cada día* de trabajo
> su *ganarás el pan*, su triste guerra,
> su ropa de oro el rico, el coronel su espada,
> su pie cansado el pobre, su maleta el viajante,
> su impecable corbata el camarero,

---

30. "Aboard the 'Uso di mare' departed the 3rd of January 1959 from Valparaiso. We're going to Venezuela. Arthritis in both ankles!"

el banquero su jaula, su uniforme el gendarme,
su convento la monja, su naranja el frutero,
su carne el carnicero, el olor de farmacia
el farmacéutico, su oficio la ramera."[31]

POEM 19

A typed version of this poem, dated to June 1968 in Isla Negra,
was found in a filing cabinet with conference papers, prologues,
and various other writings. A handwritten version was acquired
from a private individual. Here, we believe Neruda refers to the
figureheads *Jenny Lind* and *Henry Morgan,* which appear in a text
he wrote for the TV series *Historia y geografía de Pablo Neruda*
(History and geography with Pablo Neruda) in 1970.[32] If this is
the case, it seems strange that he would alter their names, although
the poem is quite cryptic in general, especially in the last two lines:
"Hay que ver lo que trae el agua / por el río de cuatro brazos!"[33]

In 1968, Neruda wrote his *World's End*. The landscape of this
poem—the river that collects "los fermentos de las fabelas / y
las máscaras del espanto"[34] that can lead "hacia el mar o hacia el
infierno"[35]—has something of the apocalyptic within it.

---

31. "Man also says / he hates his *each and every day* of work, / his *you
    shall earn the bread*, his sad war, / the rich one his clothes of gold,
    the colonel his sword, / the poor one his tired foot, the traveler
    his suitcase, / the waiter his impeccable tie, / the banker his cage,
    the gendarme his uniform, / the monk his monastery, the grocer
    his orange, / the butcher his meat, the pharmacist / the odor of
    pharmacy, the whore her profession" (Translated by William O'Daly.)

32. Please see Forrest Gander's Prologue for another interpretation.

33. "Just look what the water's carrying / up this four-armed river!"

34. "the ferment of the favelas / and ghoulish masks"

35. "off to sea or to hell"

This poem is dated Wednesday, January 10, 1973, in Isla Negra. It was found in a notebook in which, on the first page, the poet has written: "Comencé – en los primeros días – de Enero – 1973 (enfermo en cama, de una cadera) – Libro titulado – Defectos Escogidos y otros – poemas confidenciales."[36] This poem is the first that appears in the notebook. In the upper-left corner there is a note in what looks like Matilde's hand. It reads, "Defectos escogidos – Revisado."[37] It seems strange, then, that this poem was included neither in that collection, for which it appears to have been clearly and explicitly intended, nor in any of the other books of poetry Neruda was working on at the time, published posthumously. *Jardin de invierno* (*Winter Garden*[38]), 2000, and *El corazón amarillo* (*The Yellow Heart*[39]), for example, include some of the poems from this notebook. Professor Hernán Loyola has made note of various similarities between the motifs and similes in *The Yellow Heart* and *Defectos escogidos* and those that appear in *Estravagario*, including "cierto sobretono sarcástico" (a certain sarcastic overtone).

"From isolation" is the only poem by Neruda in which the telephone plays a central role; there is no "Ode to the Telephone," for instance. As can be seen, it addresses the speaker's personal relationship to the device, which gradually encroaches on and cheapens his life: "fui corrompiéndome hasta conceder / mi oreja superior (que consagré / con inocencia a pájaros y música)

---

36. "I began – on the first days – of January – 1973 (sick in bed, with a bad hip) – Book titled – Chosen Defects and others – secret poems"

37. "Chosen Defects – Checked"

38. Copper Canyon Press (1986, 2002), translated by Wililam O'Daly.

39. Copper Canyon Press (1990, 2002), translated by William O'Daly.

/ a una prostitución de cada día, / enchufando al oído el ene-
migo / que se fue apoderando de mi ser."[40]

POEM 21

No handwritten manuscript of this poem is available. The typed
version was found in a folder with copies of "Oda al caldillo
de congrio" (Ode to conger chowder), "Oda a la cuchara"
(Ode to the spoon), "A Chile de regreso" (Back to Chile), and
"Antistrofa" (Antistrophe).

"Those two solitary men" celebrates the conquest of what
Neruda calls "el cielo inanimado" ("an inanimate heaven"). In
other poems, like *Estravagario*'s "El perezoso" (Lazybones),
Neruda responds to space travel more warily: "Continuarán
viajando cosas / de metal entre las estrellas, / subirán hombres
extenuados, / violentarán la suave luna / y allí fundarán sus
farmacias."[41]

Though the poet insisted he had no desire to move to another
planet because of his love for the earth, the Soviet Union's initial
"space race" successes led to an interest in outer space as a new
stage for his poetry.

In August 1962, while flying between Sochi and Moscow,
Neruda wrote an enthusiastic article in response to the *Vostok 3*

40. "degrading myself to the point of yielding / my superior ear (which
I consecrated / innocently to birds and music) / to this everyday
prostitution, / affixing my ear to an enemy / trying to take control
of my being"

41. "They'll keep wandering, things made of / metal among the stars, /
worn-out men will go up / to desecrate the gentle moon / and there,
they'll set up their drugstores."

and *Vostok 4* missions, piloted by Andriyan Nikolayev and Pavel Popóvich. In it, he notes that "la poesía tiene que buscar nuevas palabras para hablar de estas cosas,"[42] and goes on to tell the story of a recent visit to Moscow, during which he saw for the first time a dictionary of nuclear physics terms. "Me asombré" he writes,

> porque, fuera de la palabra *átomo, reactor*, y otras pocas, no conocía ninguna de las muchas que llenan como columnas cerradas este libro singular. Las que leí y que no comprendí me paracieron palabras claramente poéticas, absolutamente necesarias a las nuevas odas, a los futuros cantos, a la poesía que relacionará de modo más estrecho al hombre de hoy con el espacio desconocido.[...] Estos dos cosmonautas que se comunican entre sí, que son examinados y dirigidos desde nuestro planeta lejano, que duermen y comen en el cosmos desconocido son los poetas descubridores del mundo.[43]

---

42. "poetry must search for new words to talk about these things"

43. "I was stunned, because, aside from *atom, reactor,* and a few others, I knew none of the words in that strange book's definitional columns. Those that I read and didn't understand seemed, to me, unmistakably poetic, absolutely fundamental to the new odes, the future cantos, to a poetry that would put modern man into closer contact with outer space.... Those two astronauts who communicate with one another, who are watched over and directed from our distant planet, who eat and sleep in the unmapped cosmos, are the poet-discoverers of the world." (*El Siglo*, Santiago, Chile, August 18, 1962.)

Neruda imagined what his planet looked like from above. On one occasion, he asked the cosmonaut Gherman Titov whether Chile was visible from space. Titov recalled seeing a range of very tall, yellow mountains and guessed that perhaps that had been Chile.

In one of his prose pieces, "Escarabagia dispersa" (Scattered Scarabistic) from April 1968, he notes, "Y aunque Leonov no me lo dijo cuando pasó por mi casa de Isla Negra, estoy seguro de que vio la Tierra desde lejos como si fuera un gran coleóptero, azulado y volante."[44] The Russian cosmonaut Alexei Leonov, who completed the first spacewalk in 1965, was another of Neruda's guides in his exploration of the skies. The poet was impressed that Leonov was also a painter. In a speech he recalled the cosmonaut telling him that "los colores del Cosmos son resplandecientes,"[45] and that no paint existed that could render them on Earth. In "El astronauta," the tenth section of *La barcarola,* Neruda imagines a poetic journey into space: "Llegué porque me invitaron a una estrella recién abierta: / ya Leonov me había dicho que cruzaríamos colores / de azufre inmenso y amaranto, fuego furioso de turquesa, / zonas insólitas de plata como espejos efervescentes."[46]

Valentina Tereshkova also made an impression on the poet. In the speech cited above, Neruda said the journeys to the cosmos had been incomplete "sin que una mujer fuera y volviera de allá

---

44. "And although Leonov didn't tell me when he passed over my house in Isla Negra, I'm sure he saw Earth from afar as if it were a great beetle, azure and flying."

45. "the colors of the cosmos are dazzling"

46. "I went because they invited me to a newly opened star: / Leonov had told me before that we would cross colors / of immense sulfur and amaranth, livid turquoise fire, / strange belts of silver like effervescent mirrors."

arriba. Y esa fue la bella cosmonauta Valentina."[47] In *Comiendo en Hungría* (Eating in Hungary), he writes that some croquettes he was served at the restaurant El Ciervo de Oro should be brought to Mars, and adds, "Entre croquetas y Valentinas engatusaríamos a los habitantes galaxianos y de repente, en un domingo cualquiera, veríamos asaltado El Ciervo de Oro por golosos extraplanetarios."[48]

DARÍO OSES

TRANSLATED BY LIZZIE DAVIS

---

47. "until a woman went and came back from there. And the one who did it was the beautiful cosmonaut Valentina."

48. "Between croquettes and Valentinas, we would sweet-talk the extraterrestrials, and then suddenly, on some Sunday, El Ciervo de Oro would be attacked by gluttons from another planet."

ABOUT THE AUTHOR

PABLO NERUDA was born Neftalí Ricardo Reyes Basoalto in Parral, Chile, in 1904. He served as consul in Burma and held diplomatic posts in various East Asian and European countries. In 1945, a few years after he joined the Communist Party, Neruda was elected to the Chilean Senate. Shortly thereafter, when Chile's political climate took a sudden turn to the right, Neruda fled to Mexico, and lived as an exile for several years. He later established a permanent home at Isla Negra. In 1970 he was appointed as Chile's ambassador to France, and in 1971 he was awarded the Nobel Prize in Literature. He authored dozens of books of poetry and prose, including over 600 poems. Neruda died in 1973.

ABOUT THE TRANSLATORS

FORREST GANDER, a writer and translator with degrees in geology and literature, was born in the Mojave Desert and grew up in Virginia. Among his most recent books are the novel *The Trace,* the series of poems *Eiko & Koma,* and two anthologies, *Panic Cure: Poetry from Spain for the 21st Century* and *Pinholes in the Night: Essential Poems from Latin America.* Gander's book *Core Samples from the World* was a finalist for the Pulitzer Prize and the National Book Critics Circle Award. He's the recipient of grants from the Library of Congress, from the Guggenheim, Howard, and Whiting Foundations, and from United States Artists. Gander is the A.K. Seaver Professor of Literary Arts & Comparative Literature at Brown University.

LIZZIE DAVIS is a writer and translator living in Madrid. Her translations from the Spanish include Elena Medel's *My First Bikini* (Jai-Alai Books, 2015) and Pilar Fraile Amador's *Circular* (Skat Editores, 2015). Her work has appeared in *The Brooklyn Rail, Asymptote, Words Without Borders,* and *a Perimeter,* among others.

THANK YOU!

The book you are holding is a testament to the diverse community of passionate readers who supported the Lost Poems of Pablo Neruda Project.

Copper Canyon Press is deeply grateful to the following individuals around the world whose philanthropic vision and love of poetry made this legacy collection possible. We have published *Then Come Back* together.

Nancy and Craig Abramson • David Adès • Kelli Russell Agodon • Lylianna Marie Allala • Roseanna Almaee • Stephen S. Alpert • Janeen Armstrong • Paul-Marie T. Arpaia • James Arthur and Shannon Robinson • Roberto Ascalon • Paul Assey • Libby Atkins and Martha Trolin • Bruce Atkinson • Margot Atwell • Aurora-Marina • Peter Badame • Rebecca Bahr • Mr. Mark Edward Bands • Thomas Charles Barnes • Caesar Ben Basan Barona • Veronica Jane and Parker Neale Barrett • Hathaway Barry • Matt and Laura Barry • Joshua D. Bartman • Ellen Bass • Johnny E. Bates, M.D. • Gary Becker • Joseph Bednarik • Mark Behr (1963–2015) • Donna and Matt Bellew • Brian Belmont • Che Ben • Magda Benavidez • Meryem of the Bensouda • David Bentley • Kitty Bergel • Lilian Bergsma–Lefever • David E. Berkowitz • Ariane Bernard • Deborah Smith Bernstein • Jordan Michael Berson • Dicken Bettinger • Jeffrey and Jill Bishop • Roger Blanton • John Blotzer • Nathalie Boisard-Beudin • Barbara Elizabeth Bolles • Twanna P. Bolling • Carla Bolt • Baby Bontongola • David Bottoms • Calvin Bowman • Annie Boyd • Adriann Braiker • Richard A. Brait • John Branch • Jeanette Brauner • David Brewster and Mary Kay Sneeringer • Althea Brimm • Rofel Brion • Louise Brown • Diana Broze • David and Kristi Buck • Vincent and Jane Buck • Courtney Buoncore • Jennifer Burgess • Kathleen Burgess • Joanna Burke • Mark A. Burke • Bill Burns • Dan Burns • Dan Burstein • Colleen Morton Busch • Trent Busch • William Cahill • Dori Cahn and Jay Stansell • Alfred E. Cambridge Jr. • Janelle Camlic • Carolee Campbell • William Lou Cardenas • J. Morgan Carney • Charles Carr • James D. Carraway • Andrew

G. Carrigan • Antonio S. Caruso • Kimberly Casey • Bonnie Cauble, and William and Elliot Hall • Cordell Caudron • Tim and Sarah Cavanaugh • Richard Cencini • David Lars Chamberlain • Simon Chappell • Sarah Charters • Bryan Chennault • Sam Chernak • Ellen W. Chu • Hans Chui • Christopher Reed Clark • Tom and Brooke Clarke • Maggie Cleveland and Jake Hasson • Philip Clum • Dorothy J. Coakley • Donald and Loryne Coffin • Allen Cohen • Quentin Cole • Colin and Jo • Elisabeth H. Colt • Lance Conn • Elena Cooper • Marsha Cooper • Keith Cowan and Linda Walsh • Tonaya Craft • Bridget Culligan • Betsey Curran, Pete Curran, and Jonathan King • Sharon D. • Andrea Michelle Davidson • Jeri Davis • Lauren Davis • Scott Davis • Page Dawsey • Alyssa DeCaulp • Eric L. Deitchman • Kiran Desai • Bill de Veas • David H. de Weese • Rachel Ann Dickenson • Victor Donozo III • Terry Drayton • John Duffy and Eileen Kiera • Duygu and Dwayne • Vasiliki Dwyer • Heather Michaela Earp • Catherine Edwards • Cara Ehlenfeldt • Kathleen Ehman • Dianne Elliott • Elaina Ellis and Ash Goddard • Jane Ellis and Jack Litewka • Steven Ellis • Jonathan Engeln, Martine Lambinet, and Sophie F. Lacson • The Entrekin Family Foundation • Sarah and Owen Fairbank • Dennis Falberg • Jeremy Falletta • Patricia Farmer • Lee Faulkner • Veronica Fernandez • Beroz Ferrell and Siegi Ranacher • Julia Ann Fetzer • Jay Fier • José Angel Figueroa • William Fisher • Pamela Fletcher • Ayame Flint • Kelly Forsythe • Agnes Fowler • Julie Fowler • Bob and Kathy Francis • Howard Franklin • Carmen R. Fuentes-Steckline, M.D. • Jerry Fulks and Stephanie Saland • Monbill Fung • John David Gabriel and Elizabeth Anne Hin • Marilyn Gabriel • Edwin and Mary Gaitan • Paul Gallipeo • Laura Gamache • Fabio Gambini y Pamela Mondino • Forrest Gander • Carlos M. Garcia and Ana Walker-Garcia • Lisha Adela García • Alan Gartenhaus and Rhoady Lee • Loretta Gase • Mimi Gardner Gates • Gwen and Patrice Gaudefroy-Demombynes • Laura Gee • Lena Georgas • Daniel Gerber • Linda Gerrard and Walter Parsons • Dale D. Goble and Susan J. Kilgore • Rafael Gonzalez-Pardo • Nathalie Grayson • Lucas Greb • Mark Greenwood • Greg LOVES Blanca • Kaitlin Heather Gregory-Cauchon • Chad E. Griswald • Michelle and Robert Grondine • Fernando Gros • Nikola Janina Guht • Agnes Gund • Deborah Gunn • Richard Guthrie • Mark Hamilton and Suzie Rapp • Mary Elizabeth Handy • Art Hanlon • Dandan Hansen • Adam Hare • Cerentha Harris • Joseph Harris • Tom Hawkins • Racine Heacox • Victoria Henige • Martha T. Heyneman • Fred Hochberg and Tom Healy • Elizabeth Hoile • Holly and Washington • Alanah Louise Horsten • Kelly Riggle Hower • Amy Hubbard • Russel Hunter, D.V.M. • Cornelia N. Hutt • Jack F. Ingram Jr. • Barbara Insel • Tina Jacobson and John Kucher • Karie Jane • Kate Janeway and Howard S. Wright • Rick Janisse •

Thomas and Cherryl Janisse • Ron Janssen • Sarah Jenkin-Hall • Duane Kirby Jensen • Marylee Jeria con amor a Marcus Cuellar • Horton A. Johnson • Kyle Johnson and Judith Kindler • Selena Jorgensen • Yves Joris, Lettergoesting • Pat Juell • Timothy J. Jursak • Victoria Kaplan • Elizabeth Smith Kara • Mary Kelley • Mary Lou Kelley • Gaylord Kellogg • Amy S. Kennedy • Janine Tamara Kessel • Gordon Khoo • Natalie Kim • Mark Kindt • April King and Nizar Ahmed • Christina King • Will and Erica Martinez Kinsey • Kinsley, Grayson, and Preston • Margaret Kirk • Mary Jane Knecht • Tricia Knoll • George Knotek • Алексей Ковалёв • Andrew L. Ko • Taroh Kogure • Despina Kotis • Phil Kovacevich and Eric Wechsler • Natasha Kraal • Fritz Kräuchi • Carolyn Kreiter-Foronda • Adam L. Kress • John Eric Ladd • Miss Linh Thi Lam • Andrew Lamantia • Christina Land • Randall Lane • Jean-Jacques (J.J.) Larrea • Ron Larsen • Linda and David Laundra • Morten Lauridsen • James V. Lawry • Rebecca Jill Leaver • Chan Y. Lee • Jeanne Marie Lee • Maureen Lee and Mark Busto • Olivia Lee • Sharon Lee • Corinne Lenk • Alexander E. Lessard • Stewart A. Levin and Diane Rothman Levin • Martin Levine • Greg Lewis • Jayne Lindley • Ariane Lopez-Huici • Joyce A.E. Loubere • Laura Lundgren • Carter Lydia • L. Lynch • Lynne • Kevin and Cristin Lyons • Shagran M. • Kelly Jo MacArthur • Alison Maclennan • Jaclyn Madden • Magaly and Lolek • René Maldonado • Ciaran Max Mandel • Brian Marsh • Lynn Martin • Vincent Masi • Gigi Mathew • W.D. Matthews • Tim Mayo • James McCorkle • Maren McDowell • JoAnne McFarland • Lyndsey M. McGrath • Laura McLane • Tanya and Michael McManus • James McNeel • Phillippe and Marian Meany • Allen K. Mears • Michael Luis Medrano • Edgar Mendelsohn • Senofer Ewing Mendoza • Nancy Mercer • Linda Merinoff • Bettie Anne Mikosinski • Hugh Miller • Matthew Clay Mills • Mina, Sergei, and Antoine • Mischa • Hayes Mizell • Christopher James Molenaar • Joann Moreno • Marissa Morquecho • Joseph P. Morra • Jay Morris • Steve and Heather Murch • Joan L. Murphy • Regina Murray • Luiza Mussnich • Leonardo Nava • Elaine and Gary Nelson • Scott Nelson • Gail Newman • Matthew Nienow • Michael Nipert • Wendy Nordquist and Phil Dinsmore • David Novros • Eric and Rhonda Obert • Eugene O'Brien • Michael O'Brien • Raymond Z. Ortiz • Kathy and Geoff Osler • Mary Pat Osterhaus • Jackie M. Ostrowicki • E. Owings • Connie Ozer • Penny and Jerry Peabody • Andrew Pearson • Samuel and Alice Peralta • Wendy Perdue • John Phillips and Anne O'Donnell • Valerie Piriak • Walter Pirie • Arlene Plevin • Julian O. Poblete • Victoria Poling • Richard Polsky • Frank Pommersheim • John and Kathy Popko • Anne Pound • P.M. • Todd Presley and Rand Dadasovich • J. Scott Price • A. Issac Pulver • Kathleen Quinn & David

Whitwell • Larry Rafferty • Geila Rajaee • Lynn Rauch • L.H. Bravo Rebolledo • Carrie Folkman Reckling • Judyth Reichenberg • W. Garrett Reynolds • Dr. Caren Rich • Margaret Riddle • Henry Ridgeway • Sally Ripamonti • Juan Carlos and Jean Marie Riquelme • Thomas Robbins • Joseph C. Roberts • Sally Rodgers • Ernesto Cuauhtémoc Sánchez Rodríguez • Kayla Romanelli • Frank Rossini and Lynn Nakamura • Wayne Roth and Kathleen Alcala • Chris Rothman and Ran Bullard • Pablo Augustine Casimer Rotter • Larry Rouch • Juliet Rowland • Stephen Rowley • Chanda Alvaro Rozumski • Ginny Ruffner • Beverly Saling • James Richard Sampel • Cherie Savy • Lee Scheingold • Kate Schilling • Pablo Tell Schreiber • Pat Schrepel • Fiona Scott • Cynthia Sears and Frank Buxton • Kim and Jeff Seely • Xiaozhi Shao • Michael Shaw • Sandra Simonett • Rick Simonson • Anabel Blue Simotas • Claudia Skelton • David E. and Catherine Eaton Skinner • Caitlin Smethurst • Annette and Paul Smith • Brenda Pauline Smith • Sandra Sohr • Roberta J. Sosa • Lance Spring • Byron Springer • Randy Squires • Evelyn Stateler • Ray and Nancy Steinberg • Jessica L. Stocks • Robert C. Stone • Amber Dorko Stopper, Tucker James Collins, Claudia Levin Dorko, and Bela Levin Dorko • W. Gene Story • Timothy Stotz, Nicole Michelle Tully, and Zoë Delphine Tully Stotz • Winnie Stratton • Natalie Strawbridge • Judith Stubenvoll • Randy Sturgis • George and Kim Suyama • Benjamin Tan and Lewis Keyte • Daphne Tann • Dale Temple • Barbara Earl Thomas • Thomas A. Thomas • Siolo Thompson • Karen Thomson • James K. Tinsley Jr. • Judith Tobin • A.M. Tolis • Diane Tomhave and Sherman Alexie • Christopher Tonniges • Elizabeth Carter Torrey • Sophia Antoinette Trapp • Stephen and Ann Treacy • Jules Bhodi Tree • William and Ruth True • Marge Tubalkain • Jac Turlings • Tom Van Buren • C. van Leeuwen • Kristen Vargas • Jose Vazquez • Yasmil Raymond Ventura • Vermont Studio Center • John Joseph Vidaurrázaga • Marlene and Bernard Vidibor • Kate Vrijmoet • John Waclawski • Dan Waggoner • Colin Walker • Christian H. Wallace • Shane Israel Wallace • Marilyn Wallner • Justin J. Walsh • Thomas Walsh • Austin Walters • Emily Warn • Burton Watson • Bailey Weems • Viola Weinberg • Debrielle Welch • Chrisi West • Charles Whatley • Madeline J. White • Precious Whittaker • Jim and Mary Lou Wickwire • Michael Wiegers • Roger C. Wilbur • Madeleine Wilde • Eran Williams • Leslie A. Wilson • Noel Wingard • John Winkelman • Warren Woessner • Sholeh Wolpé • Sara and Ted Woolsey• Mark Worthington • Joan and Craig Wrench • Bill Wu • Corrie and Ted Yackulic • Candice Baker Yacono • Yee Cang Ling • Lorin Yin • Caleb Young • Alexander Zawalnyski • Niesha Ziehmke • Barry Ziker and Margaret Chillingworth • Federico Elgueta Zunino

PABLO NERUDA BOOKS
FROM COPPER CANYON
PRESS

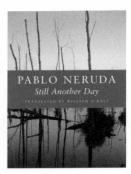

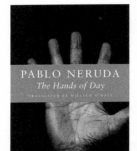

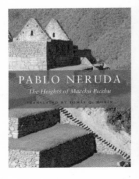

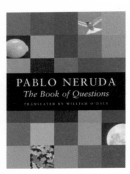

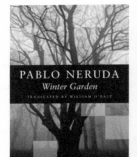